Leopard Torto

CW00539428

Leopard Tortoise as Pets

Leopard Tortoise Care, Behavior, Diet, Interaction, Costs and Health.

By

Ben Team

Table of Contents

About the Author

The author, Ben Team, is an environmental educator and author with over 16 years of professional reptile-keeping experience.

Ben currently maintains www.FootstepsInTheForest.com, where he shares information, narration and observations of the natural world.

Foreword

Picking a good pet reptile requires you to consider a variety of different things. You'll need to think about the size, personality and price of your new pet, as well as their dietary, space and thermal requirements. It is also important to think carefully about your skill set before making your choice, as some reptiles are likely to thrive in the hands of novices, while others rarely survive the mistakes new keepers often make.

If you proceed deliberately, you'll likely end up with an excellent pet for your lifestyle; if you do not, you'll probably suffer through one headache after another, as you struggle to care for a creature that is not suitable for you.

However, every potential keeper's circumstances are different, so there is no quick-and-easy way to determine a pet for yourself. Accordingly, you'll simply need to research a variety of different species, until you happen upon one that seems like a good fit.

Leopard tortoises are a great fit for many keepers, and they deserve serious consideration from those who'd like to have a tortoise as a pet.

They grow rather large, so you'll need a great deal of space to accommodate them, but panther tortoises are typically much smaller than gigantic species, such as sulcata tortoises. They also require a relatively warm and dry environment, so your geographic location will play a role in your decision, if you intend to keep your leopard tortoise outdoors.

Like all other reptiles, leopard tortoises require a rather specific diet, and some of the types of items they need can be difficult to obtain. Additionally, it can be a bit of a hassle to take a 30-pound tortoise into the vet.

If you think that a leopard tortoise may be a good fit for you, read on to learn more about their biology, natural history and the care they require to thrive in captivity.

If you are able to provide a leopard tortoise with the things it will need, you are sure to find them to be very satisfying pets, who can provide enjoyment for decades to come.

PART I: THE LEOPARD TORTOISE

Properly caring for any animal requires an understanding of the species and its place in the natural world. This includes digesting subjects as disparate as anatomy and ecology, diet and geography, and reproduction and physiology.

It is only by learning what your pet is, how it lives, what it does that you can achieve the primary goal of animal husbandry: Providing your pet with the highest quality of life possible.

Chapter 1: Leopard Tortoise Description and Anatomy

Leopard tortoises (*Stigmochelys pardalis*) are physically similar to most other tortoises, and they share a number of morphological traits with their relatives, which are unique in the Animal Kingdom.

Size

Leopard tortoises are medium to large turtles, who reach a maximum length of about 28 inches (70 centimeters). However, most are smaller, and they average about 16 inches (40 centimeters) in length.

Adult leopard tortoises weigh up to about 80 pounds (36 kilograms), although most are much smaller than this and weigh about 30 pounds (14 kilograms).

At the time of hatching, most leopard tortoises measure about 2 inches in length (5 centimeters) and weigh about 0.7 to 1 ounce (20 to 30 grams.

Sexually based size differences vary among leopard tortoise populations. Typically, females outgrow males (both in terms of growth rate and ultimate size), but the opposite trend occurs in some locations.

Color and Pattern

The leopard tortoise is an attractive animal. Their carapaces are largely straw-colored, with a variety of dark brown to black markings (consisting of a mixture of spots, splotches and lines) on top of the lighter ground color.

The amount of markings present varies wildly between different individuals (and likely between different populations), with some being heavily patterned and others having very few markings. Some individuals also feature reddish brown markings on their shells.

Leopard tortoises have yellow, brown or straw-colored skin. Some of the scales on the front legs are enlarged and plate-like, but not to the extent seen on some other tortoises, such as African spurred tortoises (*Centrochelys sulcata*).

The plastron of leopard tortoises is highly variable, although most are cream or straw-colored, with numerous dark markings. However, they are usually not as heavily marked as the carapaces of these turtles are.

Shell and General Body Plan

Leopard tortoise are oval in shape when viewed from above, but they are rounder than many other species, such as red-footed tortoise (*Chelonoidis carbonaria*), which are rather elongated.

The shells of leopard tortoises form from the fusion of dermal bones, which originate within the tortoise's skin, with the ribs and spine. Scale-like structures called scutes cover the top of this bony, box-like frame. Scutes are composed of keratin -- the same substance that forms human fingernails and hair.

The top portion of the shell is called the carapace, while the bottom portion of the shell is called the plastron. The scutes that encircle the shell's rim are called marginal scutes. Leopard tortoises have 13 dorsal scutes, 14 ventral scutes and 23 marginal scutes. There is no hinge on the shell of leopard tortoises, as there is with some chelonians.

The Head

The heads of leopard tortoises hold two large eyes. Like most turtles, leopard tortoises possess good eyesight, and rely on it (along with their sense of smell) for finding food. Like all other living turtles, leopard tortoises have no teeth; instead, they use their sharp, beak-like mouths to cut and tear food into pieces small enough for swallowing.

Leopard tortoises have no external ear opening, and while they do react to auditory stimuli, they probably do not hear very well. Most turtles are mute, but some tortoises – including male leopard tortoises – make high-pitched grunting or clucking sounds while courting or breeding females. Leopard tortoises have two nostrils on the front of their head, and they possess a good sense of smell. Tortoises, like most other vertebrates, can breathe through both their nostrils and mouth.

Limbs and Feet

Leopard tortoises have four strong legs that are well adapted for hauling their heavy bodies through the habitat. Called elephantine feet, these strong, pillar-like legs are an important adaptation for animals that must transport such massive skeletons. The front feet of leopard tortoises bear five nails, while the rear feet have four.

Tail

While male and female leopard tortoises have tails of different shapes – those of males are much longer than females and feature a different positioning of the vent – neither of the sexes have especially long tails.

Internal Organs

Internally, leopard tortoises feature anatomy that is largely similar to that of other terrestrial vertebrates, and contains largely the same basic systems. The skeletal and muscular systems of leopard tortoises provide them with structure and the capacity for movement.

Their digestive and excretory systems nourish their bodies, while their endocrine and exocrine systems produce hormones and other substances to ensure their bodies function normally. Their nervous systems transmit information and control the movements of their bodies.

The skeleton of leopard tortoises resembles those of other four-legged vertebrates, aside from the drastically modified spine and ribs. Additionally, tortoises possess anatomical modifications, such as modifications to the bones of the shoulders and pelvis, which allow them to pack most of their body inside their rib cages – a condition unique to chelonians.

Turtles breathe air, just as all other reptiles do. They inhale air through the lungs or mouth, where it travels via the windpipe or trachea to a pair of lungs. The tracheas of turtles are longer than those of similarly sized vertebrates because air has to travel the length of their relatively long necks. In the lungs, the turtles oxygenate the blood and remove the carbon dioxide that it is carrying, at which point it can be exhaled through the mouth or nose.

However, the pulmonary system of turtles does have one key difference from those of birds and mammals – reptiles lack a diaphragm. The diaphragms of birds and mammals pump air into and out of the lungs, while reptiles use muscles attached to the ribs to help pump air into and out of the lungs.

Animals such as lizards and snakes move their ribs, which in turn pump air into and out of the lungs. However, turtles and tortoises cannot move their ribs, as the ribs are attached to their rigid shells. Turtles and tortoises overcame this problem by evolving sheets of muscle within their ribs, which alternately contract and relax to force air into or out of the lungs. Additionally, when turtles move their legs it can create a pumping effect in the lungs as well, which increases the rate of air exchange.

The circulatory system of leopard tortoises and other turtles is largely similar to those of other vertebrates. The heart pumps blood to the body's various tissues by using a circuit of arteries, veins and capillaries. However, in contrast to mammals and birds, turtles have a three-, rather than four-, chambered heart. Turtle hearts have a left atrium, a right atrium and a single ventricle.

Three-chambered hearts are not as efficient at keeping oxygen-rich blood separate from oxygen-depleted blood. However, turtles have overcome this in part by evolving a muscular septum that partially separates the ventricle into two halves. This improves the efficiency of the heart somewhat, but still limits the aerobic capacity of turtles, meaning that they tire quickly after strenuous activity.

The digestive systems of leopard tortoises and their kin are similar to those of other vertebrates, but there are a few exceptions. The stomachs of turtles usually reside significantly to the left of their midline, and the intestines are compressed into a small amount of space. The process by which turtles handle nitrogenous waste differs from that of mammals, but anatomically, the kidneys and urinary tract are largely similar to the familiar system found in mammals. However, in reptiles, the urinary by-products are excreted via a structure termed the cloaca. The cloaca is a shared chamber, into which the digestive, urinary and reproductive tracts empty.

While the nervous system of leopard tortoises follows the same basic plan as is found in other vertebrates, tortoises are noteworthy for having very small brains. Usually, the brain of a tortoise is less than one percent of its total mass.

Reproductive Organs

The gonads of male turtles and tortoises are rather similar to the ones found in mammals, but they are held internally. Male turtles produce sperm in their testes and use a phallus, which arises as an outgrowth of the cloacal wall, to implant sperm in a female's cloaca. The phallus is held inside the cloaca until it is time for mating.

Female tortoises produce ova in their ovaries; after release and fertilization, the eggs settle into a structure termed the oviduct to complete their development. At this time, the mother's body begins placing calcium around the ova to establish their shells. When the eggs are ready for deposition, they are passed through the female's cloaca, one at a time.

Chapter 2: Leopard Tortoise Biology and Behavior

Like all other animals, leopard tortoises exhibit a number of biological and behavioral adaptations that allow them to survive in their natural habitats. It is important to familiarize yourself with these adaptations, so that you can provide the best possible care for your new pet.

Growth and Lifespan

Leopard tortoises are slow growing, and it takes them about a decade to mature. In captivity, they add about 2 to 4 inches of growth each year when provided with ideal conditions. By the time most leopard tortoises are 3 years old, they weigh about 2 pounds (1 kilogram) and measure about 6 to 8 inches in length.

It is possible to achieve more rapid growth by feeding animal protein, but this is a questionable practice that usually results in nutritional problems later in life.

Assuming they survive the first few years of life, leopard tortoises probably live for about 40 to 50 years in the wild, and possibly much longer. Illness, parasites and predators are the primary causes of mortality for wild-living leopard tortoises. Because these things can be treated and avoided in captivity, pet tortoise may live even longer.

Shedding

Like most other reptiles, leopard tortoises shed their skin; however, unlike snakes and lizards, who shed all of their scales at the same time, leopard tortoises shed on a rather continual basis. Because they replace very small pieces of skin at a time, the process is not terribly obvious.

Additionally, most turtles and tortoises replace and shed the scutes covering their shells regularly. New keratin scutes are added from the bottom, as the outermost (and oldest) scutes fall off.

Turtles do not, as is commonly supposed, shed their entire shell to grow a new one on a periodic basis.

Metabolism and Digestion

Leopard tortoises are ectothermic ("cold-blooded") animals, whose internal metabolism depends on their body temperature. When they are warm, their bodily functions proceed more rapidly; but when they are cold, their bodily functions proceed slowly.

This also means that leopard tortoises digest more effectively at suitably warm temperatures than they do at suboptimal temperatures. Their appetites also vary with temperature, and if the temperatures drop below the preferred range, they may cease feeding entirely.

A tortoise's body temperature largely follows ambient air temperatures, but it also absorbs and reflects radiant heat, such as that coming from the sun. They try to keep their body temperature within the preferred range by employing behaviors that allow them to adjust their temperature, such as moving into the sun to warm up or retreating into a burrow to cool off.

Senses and Intelligence

Leopard tortoises possess the same senses that most other turtles do. They have reasonably good eyesight, respond to tactile stimulation readily and appear to have a strong sense of smell. However, their sense of hearing is average at best.

Turtles have a larger brain size index than most lizards and snakes do, but this does not mean they are especially intelligent. Nevertheless, leopard tortoises are able to anticipate husbandry protocols and feeding times.

Many learn to associate their keeper with food, which can lead them to approach their keeper when entering the pen or nearing the cage. Some keepers describe the behavior as "begging".

Foraging Behavior

While they may consume to odd insect, slug or earthworm, and they may nibble at a dead animal carcass from time to time, leopard tortoises are best described as herbivorous grazers. Vegetation makes up the bulk of their diet.

They find their food – primarily grasses, cactus pads and weeds – by foraging widely. They typically forage during the morning, when the temperatures are most conducive to activity.

Diel and Seasonal Activity

Like most tortoises, leopard tortoises are diurnal. In the morning, they exit their burrows and begin foraging. If the midday temperatures climb too high, they will retreat to their burrows, possibly returning to forage in the late afternoon. Note that leopard tortoises do not necessarily emerge and become active every day. They'll occasionally remain immobile for several days at a time – particularly after large meals.

Leopard tortoises may become inactive when the temperatures are too high or too low. When doing so, they will often enter a burrow, rock crevice or similar place until the temperatures become more hospitable.

Defensive Strategies and Tactics

Leopard tortoises – like most other tortoises – try to avoid detection by predators as their first line of defense. Their camouflage color patterns and slow movements help accomplish this, and they spend their time hiding when not basking, eating or engaged in breeding behavior.

But when trapped or cornered, leopard tortoises will withdraw their heads into their shell and cover their faces with their front legs. As their legs are covered in hard, protective scales, they help to provide additional protection from predators.

The shell of adult leopard tortoises is quite hard and will resist the teeth of most small predators, but the shells of young tortoises remain soft for several years following hatching. This means that they must place even more emphasis on camouflaging with their surroundings and remaining undetected by birds, lizards, rodents, snakes and other such predators.

If lifted off the ground, leopard tortoises may void the contents of their cloaca, and some individuals may attempt to bite.

Reproduction

Breeding activity can occur at any time of the year, but it is most common between May and October.

Males spend much of this time pursuing, courting and attempting to breed females. Upon seeing a potential mate, the male will initiate a sequence of dramatic head bobs. He will then approach the female from behind and begin mating with her.

Males may engage in physical bouts during this time, as they fight over resources – primarily breeding partners and territory. Females rarely exhibit antagonistic behaviors toward other females, but it has been observed on occasion.

Fertilization may follow a single mating, although pairs sometimes mate more than once in a season. Males will mate with as many females as possible.

Females often construct a 6- to 10-inch-deep nest in which they'll deposit their eggs. They may urinate on hard-packed soil to make it easier to dig the nest. Once finished, they will cover the eggs back up and tamp down the soil to camouflage the egg chamber.

Females provide no further parental care after depositing their eggs. Females often produce several different clutches over the course of the year, about 3 to 4 weeks apart.

Chapter 3: Classification and Taxonomy

The terms "turtle," "tortoise," "terrapin" and "chelonian" are not always applied consistently, and some clarification is warranted.

The term "turtle" correctly refers to all 327 currently recognized species of the order Testudines. Likewise, the term "chelonian," refers to all living turtles – this term arose from the word "Chelonia," which is an outdated name for the order. This means that the terms "turtle" and "chelonian" apply to sea turtles, leopard tortoises (*Geochelone pardalis*), red-eared sliders (*Trachemys scripta elegans*) and all of their close relatives.

The term "tortoise" applies to land-dwelling, herbivorous species of the family Testudinidae, although some people use the term to describe any terrestrial turtle. For instance, rather than calling a *Terrapene carolina* an eastern box turtle, some call it an eastern box tortoise. This is not technically correct, but it is common to encounter such usage.

The term "terrapin" applies to freshwater turtles, although it may refer specifically to one species: the diamondback terrapin (*Malaclemys terrapin*). This term is most common in the southeastern United States as well as along the Mid-Atlantic coast. In some places, the term refers to aquatic turtles that are commonly consumed by humans – in such cases; it may be applied to sliders (*Trachemys* sp.), cooters (*Pseudemys* sp.) or even common snapping turtles (*Chelydra serpentina*)

Therefore, while the name "leopard tortoise" is one of the most descriptive, informative and accurate common names for these creatures, the name "leopard turtle" is also acceptable. "leopard terrapin" is not an appropriate name for these creatures, but the generic terms turtle, tortoise and chelonian are all applicable.

Leopard Tortoise Classification
Scientists do not completely agree on the classification scheme for turtles. While scientists do agree that all turtles are related, they disagree about where their common ancestor fits in the vertebrate family tree. Some researchers are convinced by DNA-based evidence that suggests chelonians' closest relatives are animals

called archosaurs – a group that included dinosaurs and pterosaurs, but is represented by birds and crocodilians in the modern world. By contrast, other researchers find the morphological evidence more compelling, and believe that lizards are the closest relatives of turtles.

Regardless of which point of origin scientists eventually agree upon, turtles are clearly a monophyletic group, meaning that they all arose from a common ancestor. The shell of turtles is one of the most unique adaptations that any animal has ever evolved, and it is highly unlikely that this adaptation evolved more than once.

The basal split in the chelonian lineage is between those turtles whose necks fold sideways, and those whose necks retract vertically, straight back into the ribcage. Most living species have vertically retracting necks, and scientists recognize several subgroups of this group. One such group is the family Testudinidae, which contains all of the living tortoises.

Scientists divide the various tortoises of the family Testudinidae into different genera, each of which contains one or more species. Leopard tortoises are the sole members of the genus *Stigmochelys*. However, some authorities still use an older genus name for leopard tortoises: *Pardalis*. Other authorities place the species in the genus *Centrochelys*.

Although some keepers recognize two different subspecies of leopard tortoise, recent research has shown that such distinctions are without merit. Nevertheless, leopard tortoise populations vary significantly across their wide range.

Chapter 4: The Leopard Tortoise's World

To maintain a leopard tortoise successfully, you must understand the animal's native habitat and provide a reasonable facsimile of it.

Range

Leopard tortoises are found through most of the southern and eastern portions of the African continent. They are found in some part of the following countries:

- South Africa

- Namibia

- Angola

- Botswana

- Zimbabwe

- Mozambique

- Swaziland

- Lesotho

- Malawi

- Zambia

- Tanzania

- Rwanda

- Burundi

- Kenya

- South Sudan

- Uganda

- Ethiopia

- Somalia

Climate and Habitat

Most portions of the Leopard tortoise's range are warm and seasonally dry. In fact, habitat changes appear to be a limiting factor for the species' range. For example, the western borders of their range bump up into dense, tropical forests, while some of the boundary regions in the north border desert or near-desert regions.

However, there is quite a bit of variation in the climates across the vast range of this species. For example, leopard tortoises living in Western Ethiopia live in a Tropical Savannah Climate, while those living in eastern Somalia are exposed to a Warm Semi-Arid Climate. Some living in South Africa may even inhabit areas classified as Cold Dessert Climates.

Predators

Like most animals, leopard tortoises are subject to predation by several other species in their natural habitats. However, the relative risk of predation for leopard tortoises changes drastically with age; it is highest right after hatching, and drops with increasing age and size.

Young leopard tortoises may be eaten by a variety of small and medium-sized predators. This includes everything from carnivorous mammals to predatory birds to snakes. The shells of young tortoises are very soft, and they do not provide much protection.

Leopard tortoises may drink from temporary puddles.

By contrast, relatively few predators consume adult leopard tortoises. Humans probably represent the greatest threat to adult tortoises, but large cats, hyenas and canids likely consume large leopard tortoises (or portions thereof) from time to time.

PART II: LEOPARD TORTOISE HUSBANDRY

Once equipped with a basic understanding of what leopard tortoises *are* (Chapter 1 and Chapter 3), where they *live* (Chapter 4), and what they *do* (Chapter 2) you can begin learning about their captive care.

Animal husbandry is an evolving pursuit. Keepers shift their strategies frequently as they incorporate new information and ideas into their husbandry paradigms.

There are few "right" or "wrong" answers, and what works in one situation may not work in another. Accordingly, you may find that different authorities present different, and sometimes conflicting, information regarding the care of these tortoises.

In all cases, you must strive to learn as much as you can about your pet and its natural habitat, so that you may provide it with the best quality of life possible.

Chapter 5: Leopard Tortoises as Pets

Leopard tortoises can make rewarding pets, but you must know what to expect before adding one to your home and family. This includes not only understanding the nature of the care they require, but also the costs associated with this care.

Assuming that you feel confident in your ability to care for a turtle and endure the associated financial burdens, you can begin seeking your individual pet.

Understanding the Commitment

Keeping a leopard tortoise as a pet requires a substantial commitment. You will be responsible for your pet's well-being for the rest of its life. Tortoises are long-live animals, and you must be prepared to care for your new pet for many years.

Can you be sure that you will still want to care for your pet several years in the future? Do you know what your living situation will be? What changes will have occurred in your family? How will your working life have changed over this time?

You must consider all of these possibilities before acquiring a new pet. Failing to do so often leads to apathy, neglect and even resentment, which is not good for you or your pet tortoise.

Neglecting your pet is wrong, and in some locations, a criminal offense. You must continue to provide quality care for your leopard tortoise, even once the novelty has worn off, and it is no longer fun to clean the cage and prepare the fruits and vegetables he needs each week.

Once you purchase a tortoise, its well-being becomes your responsibility until it passes away at the end of a long life, or you have found someone who will agree to adopt the animal for you. Unfortunately, this is rarely an easy task. You may begin with thoughts of selling your pet to help recoup a small part of your investment, but these efforts will largely fall flat.

While professional breeders may profit from the sale of leopard tortoises, amateurs are at a decided disadvantage. Only a tiny sliver of the general population is interested in reptilian pets, and only a small subset of these are interested in keeping leopard tortoises.

Of those who are interested in acquiring a leopard tortoise, most would rather start fresh, by *purchasing* a small hatchling or juvenile from an established breeder, rather than adopting your questionable animal *for free.*

After having difficulty finding a willing party to purchase or adopt your animal, many owners try to donate their pet to a local zoo. Unfortunately, this rarely works either.

Zoos are not interested in your leopard tortoise, no matter how pretty he is. He is a pet with little to no reliable provenance and questionable health status. This is simply not the type of animal zoos are eager to add to their multi-million-dollar collections.

Zoos obtain most of their animals from other zoos and museums; failing that, they obtain their animals directly from their land of origin. As a rule, they do not accept donated pets.

No matter how difficult it becomes to find a new home for your unwanted tortoise, you must never release non-native reptiles into the wild.

Additionally, released or escaped reptiles cause a great deal of distress to those who are frightened by them. This leads local municipalities to adopt pet restrictions or ban reptile keeping entirely.

The Costs of Captivity
Reptiles are often marketed as low-cost pets. While true in a relative sense (the costs associated with dog, cat, horse or tropical fish husbandry are often much higher than they are for leopard tortoises), potential keepers must still prepare for the financial implications of tortoise ownership.

At the outset, you must budget for the acquisition of your pet, as well as the costs of purchasing or constructing a habitat. Unfortunately, while many keepers plan for these costs, they typically fail to consider the on-going costs, which will quickly eclipse the initial startup costs.

Startup Costs

One surprising fact most new keepers learn is the enclosure and equipment will often cost as much as (or more than) the animal does (except in the case of very high-priced specimens).

Prices fluctuate from one market to the next, but in general, the least you will spend on a healthy leopard tortoise is about $150 (£110), while the least you will spend on the *initial* habitat and assorted equipment will be about $50 (£40). Replacement equipment and food will represent additional (and ongoing) expenses.

Examine the charts on the following pages to get an idea of three different pricing scenarios. While the specific prices listed will vary based on innumerable factors, the charts are instructive for first-time buyers.

The first scenario details a budget-minded keeper, trying to spend as little as possible. The second example estimates the costs for a keeper with a moderate budget, and the third example provides a case study for extravagant shoppers, who want an expensive tortoise and top-notch equipment.

These charts are only provided estimates; your experience may vary based on a variety of factors.

Inexpensive Option

Hatchling Leopard Tortoise	$150 (£110)
Economy Homemade Habitat	$50 (£38)
Light Fixtures and Bulbs	$50 (£38)
Plants, Substrate, Hides, etc.	$20 (£15)
Infrared Thermometer	$35 (£27)
Digital Indoor-Outdoor Thermometer	$20 (£15)
Water Dish, Food Dishes, Spray Bottles, Misc.	$20 (£15)
Total	**$345 (£258)**

Moderate Option

Adult Leopard Tortoise	$300 (£220)
Premium Homemade Habitat	$100 (£76)
Light Fixtures and Bulbs	$50 (£38)
Plants, Substrate, Hides, etc.	$20 (£16)
Infrared Thermometer	$35 (£27)
Digital Indoor-Outdoor Thermometer	$20 (£16)
Water Dish, Food Dishes, Spray Bottles, Misc.	$20 (£16)
Total	**$545 (£409)**

Premium Option

Adult Lepoard Tortoise Colony	$1000 (£735)
Premium Commercial Cage	$500 (£383)
Light Fixtures and Bulbs	$50 (£38)
Plants, Substrate, Hides, etc.	$20 (£15)
Infrared Thermometer	$35 (£27)
Digital Indoor-Outdoor Thermometer	$20 (£15)
Water Dish, Food Dishes, Spray Bottles, Misc.	$20 (£15)
Total	**$1,645 (£1,228)**

Ongoing Costs

The ongoing costs of leopard tortoise ownership primarily fall into one of three categories: food, maintenance and veterinary care.

Food costs are the most significant of the three, but they are relatively consistent and somewhat predictable. Some maintenance costs are easy to calculate, but things like equipment malfunctions are impossible to predict with any certainty. Veterinary expenses are hard to predict and vary wildly from one year to the next.

Food Costs

Food is the single greatest ongoing cost you will experience while caring for your leopard tortoise. To obtain a reasonable estimate of your yearly food costs, you must consider the number of meals you will feed your pet per year and the cost of each meal.

The amount of food your tortoise will consume will vary based on numerous factors, including his size, the average temperatures in his habitat and his health.

As a ballpark number, you should figure that you'll need about $5 (£4) per week – roughly $250 (£191) per year -- for food. You could certainly spend more or less than this, but that is a reasonable estimate for back-of-the-envelope calculations.

Veterinary Costs

While you should always seek veterinary advice at the first sign of illness, it is probably not wise to haul your healthy tortoise to the vet's office for no reason – they don't require "checkups" or annual vaccinations as some other pets may. Accordingly, you shouldn't incur any veterinary expenses unless your pet falls ill.

However, veterinary care can become very expensive, very quickly. In addition to a basic exam or phone consultation, your tortoise may need cultures, x-rays or other diagnostic tests performed. In light of this, wise keepers budget at least $200 to $300 (£160 to £245) each year to cover any emergency veterinary costs.

Maintenance Costs

It is important to plan for both routine and unexpected maintenance costs. Commonly used items, such as paper towels, disinfectant and top soil are rather easy to calculate. However, it is not easy to know how many burned out light bulbs, cracked misting units or faulty thermostats you will have to replace in a given year.

Those who keep their tortoise in simple enclosures will find that about $50 (£40) covers their yearly maintenance costs. By contrast, those who maintain elaborate habitats may spend $200 (£160) or more each year.

Always try to purchase frequently used supplies, such as light bulbs, paper towels and disinfectants in bulk to maximize your savings. It is often beneficial to consult with local reptile-keeping clubs, who often pool their resources to attain greater buying power.

Myths and Misunderstandings

Unfortunately, there are many myths and misunderstandings about leopard tortoises and reptile-keeping in general. Some myths represent outdated thinking or techniques, while other myths and misunderstandings reflect the desires of keepers, rather than the reality of the situation.

Myth: *Leopard tortoises will only grow to the size of their enclosure, and then they stop growing entirely.*

Fact: Despite the popularity of this myth, healthy tortoises do not stop growing until they reach their final size. Keeping a turtle in a small cage is an inhumane practice that will only lead to a stressed, sick animal.

Myth: *Leopard tortoises are reptiles, so they are not capable of suffering or feeling pain.*

Fact: While it is important to avoid anthropomorphizing, or projecting human emotions and motivations to non-human entities, reptiles – including leopard tortoises – feel pain. There is no doubt that they can experience pain and seek to avoid it. While it is impossible to know exactly what a tortoise thinks, there is no reason to believe that they do not suffer similarly to other animals, when injured, ill or depressed.

Myth: *All you have to feed a leopard tortoise is lettuce.*

Fact: No single vegetable will provide for all of the nutritional needs of leopard tortoises. In truth, iceberg lettuce is not even a good ingredient to include in tortoise diets. Leopard tortoises need a variety of high calcium, high fiber foods, including wild leaves, weeds, flowers and store-bought vegetables.

Myth: *Leopard tortoises can be allowed to roam about unsupervised.*

Fact: Leopard tortoises may get themselves into trouble if allowed to roam unsupervised. Even if allowed freedom inside a home, they may chew electrical wires, topple furniture, foul carpets or stain wood floors. If you can design a "tortoise proof" area, and ensure that it does not contain any items that may harm the tortoise, it is acceptable to allow the turtles freedom within a confined area. Leaving a leopard tortoise unsupervised outdoors courts disaster. Your tortoise may be attacked by predators, stolen, hit by a car or it may simply vanish into the local habitat.

Myth: *Leopard tortoises are adapted to temperature extremes, so it is not necessary to use a thermometer or monitor the cage temperatures.*

Fact: Leopard tortoises have evolved a wide array of adaptations that allow them to survive where few other tortoises can. However, much of the way they do this is by becoming inactive when temperatures are not conducive to activity. Leopard tortoises still require temperatures within a fairly narrow range, and as the keeper, you must monitor the habitat temperatures often to ensure the health and well-being of your pet.

Myth: *My leopard tortoise likes to be held so he can feel the warmth of my hands.*

Fact: In truth, your leopard tortoise may tolerate being held, but it probably does not "like" it. This myth springs from the notion that because reptiles are "cold blooded," and they must derive their heat from external sources, they enjoy warmth at all times. In truth, while tortoises are ectothermic or "cold blooded," they are most comfortable within a given range of temperatures. This temperature varies with the season and over the course of the day, but averages between about 75 and 85 degrees Fahrenheit (24 to 29 degrees Celsius) – your hands are actually a bit warm for the animals.

Myth: *Turtles never bite because they do not have teeth.*

Fact: While it is true that turtles and tortoises lack teeth, their beaks are often strong, hard and sharp. Turtles of about three to four inches in size can easily break human skin with a bite. While some species, such as leopard tortoises, are known for their docile, nothing precludes them from biting. To be clear: Leopard tortoises are not likely to bite their keepers, but as a keeper, you must understand that it is a possibility.

Myth: *Leopard tortoises are good pets for young children.*

Fact: While many turtles make wonderful pets for adults, teenagers and families, they require more care than a young child can provide. The age at which a child is capable of caring for a turtle will vary, but children should be about ten years of age before they are allowed to care for their own turtle. Parents must exercise prudent judgment and make a sound assessment of their child's capabilities and maturity. Children will certainly enjoy pet turtles, but they must be cared for by someone with adequate maturity. Additionally, it is important to consider the potential for young children contracting salmonella and other pathogens from the family pet.

Myth: *If you get tired of a turtle, it is easy to find a new home for it. The zoo will surely want your pet; after all, you are giving it to them free of charge! If that doesn't work, you can always just release it into the wild.*

Fact: Acquiring a pet turtle is a very big commitment. Most turtles are long lived animals, and leopard tortoises have very long lives. They reach at least 40 to 50 years of age in the wild, and they may live much longer than that in captivity. Even if you purchase a wild-caught animal that is already 30 years old, you may have to care for it for 10 or 20 more years.

If you ever decide that your tortoise no longer fits your family or lifestyle, you may have a tough time finding a suitable home for it. You can attempt to sell the animal, but this is illegal in some places, and often requires a permit or license to do legally.

Zoos and pet stores will be reticent to accept your pet – even at no charge – because they cannot be sure that your pet does not have an illness that could spread through their collections. A zoo may have to spend hundreds or thousands of dollars for the care, housing and veterinary care to accept your pet leopard tortoise, and such things are not taken lightly. While leopard tortoises are very neat animals, and they are worthy ambassadors for turtles, they are not rare nor especially sought after, by such institutions.

Some people consider releasing the tortoise into the wild if no other accommodations can be made, but such acts are destructive, often illegal and usually a death sentence for the tortoise. Released tortoises will have very little chance of surviving, and even if they do, they will never reproduce.

You will likely have to solicit the help of a rescue group or shelter devoted to reptiles in finding a new home for an unwanted tortoise.

Some leopard tortoises are darker than others.

Acquiring Your Leopard Tortoise
Modern reptile enthusiasts can acquire tortoises from a variety of sources, each with a different set of pros and cons.

Pet stores are one of the first places many people see leopard tortoises, and they become the de facto source of pets for many beginning keepers. While they do offer some unique benefits to prospective keepers, pet stores are not always the best place to purchase a tortoise; so, consider all of the available options, including breeders and reptile swap meets, before making a purchase.

Pet Stores

Pet stores offer a number of benefits to keepers shopping for leopard tortoises, including convenience: They usually stock all of the equipment your new tortoise needs, including cages, heating devices and food items.

Additionally, they offer you the chance to inspect the tortoise up close before purchase. In some cases, you may be able to choose from more than one specimen. Many pet stores provide health guarantees for a short period, which provide some recourse if your new pet turns out to be ill.

However, pet stores are not always the ideal place to purchase your new pet. Pet stores are retail establishments, and as such, you will usually pay more for your new pet than you would from a breeder.

Additionally, pet stores rarely know the pedigree of the animals they sell, and they will rarely know the tortoise's date of birth, or other pertinent information.

Other drawbacks associated with pet stores primarily relate to the staff's inexperience. While some pet stores concentrate on reptiles and may educate their staff about proper tortoise care, many others provide incorrect advice to their customers.

It is also worth considering the increased exposure to pathogens that pet store animals endure, given the constant flow of animals through such facilities.

Reptile Expos

Reptile expos offer another option for purchasing tortoises. Reptile expos often feature resellers, breeders and retailers in the same room, all selling various types of tortoises and other reptiles.

Often, the prices at such events are quite reasonable and you are often able to select from many different tortoises. However, if you have a problem, it may be difficult to find the seller after the event is over.

Breeders
Because they usually offer unparalleled information and support to their customers, breeders are generally the best place for most novices to shop for leopard tortoises. Additionally, breeders often know the species well, and are better able to help you learn the husbandry techniques necessary for success.

The primary disadvantage of buying from a breeder is that you must often make such purchases from a distance, either by phone or via the internet. Nevertheless, most established breeders are happy to provide you with photographs of the animal you will be purchasing, as well as his or her parents.

Selecting Your Leopard Tortoise
Not all leopard tortoises are created equally, so it is important to select a healthy individual that will give you the best chance of success.

Practically speaking, the most important criterion to consider is the health of the animal. However, the sex, age and history of the tortoise are also important things to consider.

Health Checklist
Always check your tortoise thoroughly for signs of injury or illness before purchasing it. If you are purchasing the animal from someone in a different part of the country, you must inspect it immediately upon delivery. Notify the seller promptly if the animal exhibits any health problems.

Avoid the temptation to acquire or accept a sick or injured animal in hopes of nursing him back to health. Not only are you likely to incur substantial veterinary costs while treating your new pet, you will likely fail in your attempts to restore the tortoise to full health. Sick animals rarely recover in the hands of novices.

Additionally, by purchasing injured or diseased animals, you incentivize poor husbandry on the part of the retailer. If retailers lose money on sick or injured animals, they will take steps to avoid this eventuality, by acquiring healthier stock in the first place, and providing better care for their charges.

As much as is possible, try to observe the following features:

- **Observe the tortoise's shell and skin**. It should be free of lacerations and other damage. Pay special attention to those areas that frequently sustain damage, such as the tip of the tail, the toes and the front of the face. A small cut or abrasion may be relatively easy to treat, but significant abrasions and cuts are likely to become infected and require significant treatment.

- **Gently check the tortoise's crevices and creases for ticks**. Avoid purchasing any animal that has ticks. Additionally, you should avoid purchasing any other animals from this source, as they are likely to harbor parasites as well.

- **Examine the tortoise's eyes, ears and nostrils**. The eyes should not be sunken, and they should be free of discharge. The nostrils should be clear and dry – tortoises with runny noses or those who blow bubbles are likely to be suffering from a respiratory infection. However, be aware that tortoises often get some water in their nostrils while drinking water. This is no cause for concern.

- **Gently palpate the animal and ensure no lumps or anomalies are apparent**. Lumps in the muscles or abdominal cavity may indicate parasites, abscesses or tumors.

- **Observe the tortoise's demeanor**. Healthy tortoises are aware of their environment and react to stimuli. When active, the animal should calmly explore his environment. Avoid lethargic animals, which do not appear alert.

- **Check the tortoise's vent**. The vent should be clean and free of smeared feces. Smeared feces can indicate parasites or bacterial infections.

- **Check the tortoise's appetite**. If possible, ask the retailer to feed the tortoise a piece of fruit or vegetable. A healthy, suitably warm animal should usually exhibit a strong food drive, although failing to eat is not *necessarily* a bad sign – the tortoise may not be hungry.

35

The Age

Hatchling tortoises are very fragile until they reach about one month of age. Before this, they are unlikely to thrive in the hands of beginning keepers.

Accordingly, most beginners should purchase two- or three-month-old juveniles, who have already become well established. Animals of this age tolerate the changes associated with a new home better than very young specimens do. Further, given their larger size, they will better tolerate temperature and humidity extremes than smaller animals will.

The Sex

Unless you are attempting to breed tortoises, you should select a male pet, as females are more likely to suffer from reproduction-related health problems than males are.

Many females will produce and deposit egg clutches upon reaching maturity, whether they are housed with a male or not. While this is not necessarily problematic, novices can easily avoid this unnecessary complication by selecting males as pets.

Quarantine

Because new animals may have illnesses or parasites that could infect the rest of your collection, it is wise to quarantine all new acquisitions. This means that you should keep any new animal as separated from the rest of your pets as possible. Only once you have ensured that the new animal is healthy should you introduce it to the rest of your collection.

During the quarantine period, you should keep the new tortoise in a simplified habitat, with a paper substrate, water bowl, basking spot and a few hiding places. Keep the temperature and humidity at ideal levels.

It is wise to obtain fecal samples from your tortoise during the quarantine period. You can take these samples to your veterinarian, who can check them for signs of internal parasites. Always treat any existing parasite infestations before removing the animal from quarantine.

Always tend to quarantined animals last, as this reduces the chances of transmitting pathogens to your healthy animals. Do not wash quarantined water bowls or cage furniture with those belonging to your healthy animals. Whenever possible, use completely separate tools for quarantined animals and those that have been in your collection for some time.

Always be sure to wash your hands thoroughly after handling quarantined animals, their cages or their tools. Particularly careful keepers wear a smock or alternative clothing when handling quarantined animals.

Quarantine new acquisitions for a minimum of 30 days; 60 or 90 days is even better. Many zoos and professional breeders maintain 180- or 360-day-long quarantine periods.

Chapter 6: Providing the Captive Habitat

In most respects, providing your leopard tortoise with a suitable captive habitat entails functionally replicating the various aspects of the habitat he'd experience in the wild.

In addition to providing your pet with an enclosure, you must provide the animal with the correct thermal environment, appropriate humidity, substrate, and suitable cage furniture.

The first thing you must decide upon when planning how to house your tortoise is whether you want to keep him indoors or outdoors.

Outdoor Caging

There are a variety of reasons why outdoor habitats are well suited for tortoises in general and leopard tortoises specifically.

Almost all tortoises benefit from basking in the unfiltered sunlight of outdoor enclosures and the larger amount of space they usually afford. Additionally, by keeping them outside, you do not have to purchase expensive lighting systems. Leopard tortoises will also benefit from the numerous wild weeds and plants that may grow right in their cage.

However, outdoor maintenance does have a few drawbacks. Outdoor maintenance is not appropriate for all climates, and your local climate must be relatively similar to that which they experience in the wild.

In order to maintain leopard tortoises outdoors, your local climate must satisfy the following conditions:

- The ambient daily temperatures must reach the mid-80s Fahrenheit (26 to 30 degrees Celsius) for several hours per day, for most of the year.

- The sunlight should be strong enough to produce basking spots with surface temperatures of at least 100 degrees Fahrenheit (37 degrees Celsius) for at least two or three hours per day.

- The climate cannot be excessively wet.

- The nighttime temperatures must not drop below about 65 to 70 degrees Fahrenheit (18 to 21 degrees Celsius).

If your local climate is not warm enough, additional heating elements can be added to the habitat, but if it is difficult to overcome the challenges presented by climates that are too hot.

If you do not live in an area with a suitable climate for consistent outdoor maintenance, you may be able to utilize outdoor caging for part of the year. If this is not feasible, it is still very beneficial to take your tortoise outside for regular "walks" in which the tortoise can bask in natural sunlight.

In addition to the local climate, several other criteria must be met in order to successfully maintain tortoises outdoors.

- Pesticides, herbicides, fertilizers and other chemicals must not be used in proximity to the habitat. Because groundwater can transport such chemicals, it is important that the habitat be buffered on all sides by several feet (meters) of chemical-free land.

- The area must be free of predators or the habitat must be able to exclude them completely. Potential predators of small leopard tortoises include foxes, raccoons, hawks, coyotes and domestic pets.

- The habitat must be installed in an area that is convenient to maintain, yet is located away from areas with high foot-traffic.

Outdoor cages vary in design, as most are custom built for the location. However, they all feature some type of walls, which create the enclosed area. Outdoor turtle habitats often resemble scaled-down versions of livestock pens. Several different materials can be used to construct the walls of the pen.

- Concrete blocks are sturdy, relatively inexpensive and easy to work with (although they are heavy). However, concrete blocks do not look very attractive, and without reinforcing them, they can topple. Further, it can be challenging to attach a roof to the top of the blocks.

- Corrugated plastic panels are lightweight, easy to work with and most animals cannot climb them. However, to be rigid enough, they must be attached to some sort of frame.

- Poured concrete walls are the best possible option, although constructing pens made of such walls is laborious and challenging. However, if you have the expertise, skill and finances to utilize poured concrete walls, they are unsurpassed in terms of utility, stability and aesthetics.

- Chain link fencing, chicken wire and similar materials are not appropriate for the pen walls. In addition to allowing some predators (such as rats) to enter the habitat, leopard tortoises may climb the material or become entangled in it, causing injury.

- Wood can be used to construct the walls, but it will need to be replaced as it rots or covered in an animal-safe sealant.

Regardless of the material used, the walls for a tortoise pen must be at least 16 to 20 inches (40 to 50 centimeters) in height. In general, the higher the walls, the safer the turtles will be, but wall height will reduce the amount of sunlight that shines into the habitat, when the sun is at a low angle. This may be a problem for keepers living at extreme latitudes.

One of the great benefits that outdoor cages provide in contrast to indoor cages is that it is usually easier to provide large accommodations for the tortoises. While it is possible to keep leopard tortoises indoors in about 16 square feet of space (1.5 square meters), it is highly desirable to provide much more space than this.

Strive for cages with 40 to 50 square feet (3.5 to 4.5 square meters) of space for up to three turtles. Larger groups necessitate even more space.

On top of the cage, it is usually desirable to place some type of cover. If the walls are smooth and adequately tall -- at least 6 feet (3 meters) -- then most predators will be excluded. However, this does nothing to stop hawks, vultures, owls and other predator birds, from snacking on the turtles. Additionally, raccoons or opossums may climb into the cage from an overhanging tree or structure.

Be sure to allow the natural, unfiltered sunlight to bathe part of the pen, so glass, plastic and opaque materials are not good choices for the lid of an outdoor habitat.

A leopard tortoise foraging in its natural habitat.

While not appropriate for the cage walls, chain link fence, chicken wire and hardware cloth are good materials for the top of an outdoor habitat. They will require some type of frame to remain in place. The lid will have to be removable unless the cage is tall enough to permit you to walk into it from the side.

Another great benefit of outdoor habitats is that they allow a deep substrate. The challenge for the keeper is providing a suitable quantity and quality of substrate, while preventing the captive from tunneling out of the cage or undermining cage props or walls.

The best substrates for leopard tortoises approximate those of their natural habitat. Usually, a mixture of one-part sand to one-part coconut fiber produces a light, well-drained mix that permits burrowing. Top soil or naturally occurring soil may be used as well, but it must be able to retain water and hold its shape when your pet tries to create a burrow.

Ensure that the habitat's walls extend about 18 to 24 (45 to 60 cm) inches below ground level to reduce the chances that your tortoise will dig under the wall and escape. Further protection can be had by attaching a 12-inch (25-centimeter) length of chicken wire or hardware cloth to the bottom of each wall panel. Place the chicken wire in the hole (which may need widening) so that it extends directly from the base of the wall to the inside of the pen. This way, if your tortoise digs down past the bottom of the wall, it will run into

41

the hardware cloth, thus blocking his attempts at tunneling to freedom.

Always be sure that outdoor habitats feature many different microclimates. Try to include flat areas that receive full morning sun, as well as places that provide deep shade to escape from the sun during the middle of the day.

Indoor Caging

Despite the appeal of outdoor caging, many people opt to keep their tortoises indoors. Indoor maintenance is possible, but the endeavor is often more difficult to execute as the keeper must replicate the sun, and space constraints are often more severe indoors.

If you have access to a basement or garage, it is possible to construct a pen for the tortoises, much as outdoor pens are constructed. Stacked cinder blocks or framed panels make suitable walls, and substrate can be placed on a liner covering the floor. For such pens, you can suspend the lights with chains attached to the ceiling. If the area is free of pets and children, no lids are necessary.

Indoor pens designed in this manner avoid one of the key challenges of indoor cages: limited cage space. Given an average sized basement or garage, 50 square feet (4.5 square meters) devoted to the turtles may only account for five percent of the total space.

If you do not have access to a place suitable for an indoor pen, you will need some type of container or cage to use for the habitat. Some containers work better than others do, and you will have to decide which type of container works best for your needs.

- Commercially produced, plastic reptile terrariums often work well, feature useful design elements (such as built-in light shrouds) and limit the work necessary to the hobbyist. However, only the largest sizes are appropriate for the maintenance of leopard tortoises.

- Glass aquariums are inappropriate for leopard tortoises. Cages of the necessary size are difficult to find locally, incredibly expensive, unmanageably heavy and fragile. Additionally, such cages generally lack sufficient ventilation for these turtles.

- Commercially produced tortoise tubs or tables are a good solution for young turtles; older turtles may require larger accommodations than such products offer. If suitably large tubs or tables are used, these cages are among the best possible options, as they are designed explicitly for turtles.

- Troughs, large tubs or prefabricated pool liners can be used as the base of your leopard tortoise habitat. Prefabricated pond liners are a cost-effective choice for the amount of size they provide, but they often come in irregular shapes. Large cattle troughs, stock tanks and home storage containers work well if they can be found in large enough sizes and appropriate configurations.

The majority of keepers elect to use a trough or large storage box to maintain their captives. This is often the most economical solution, but it is also a technically sound approach.

Troughs can be made of plastic or galvanized metal as long as they are designed to hold water for stock animals. Plastic containers are usually designed with more gradually sloping sides, while the side walls of metal troughs are usually vertical.

Troughs must have at least 8 square feet (.75 square meters) of space per inhabitant, but it is better to provide much, much more space. Consider that the recommendation for outdoor leopard tortoises is about 50 square feet (4.5 square meters) of space. In all cases, provide your tortoise with as much room as possible. In addition to providing room for exercise, it is easier to generate numerous microclimates in large cages.

While tubs and stock tanks are relatively lightweight when empty, they will become much less mobile when filled with several inches of substrate, heating devices and light fixtures. Accordingly, it can be advantageous to construct a wooden frame with casters or wheels to hold the trough. This will allow you to move it much more easily when the need most assuredly arises, such as when an object falls behind the trough.

It may be necessary to construct frames or lids to hold light fixtures or attach lids if necessary. Tortoises will rarely escape from such cages, but ill-intentioned pets or children can access the tortoises easily, if no lid is used.

Trough-like containers can be constructed from sealed wood or plastic panels. While difficult to construct and design for those not familiar with such work, it allows a great deal of flexibility for adapting the container to the room. There is no reason that the container must be square, rectangular or round.

When constructing a container, consider designing it in such a way that allows you to break down the cage annually for disinfection and repair. For example, utilize bolts and nuts, which are easy to remove, rather than nails or wood screws in construction of the enclosure.

Animals Per Enclosure

Often, keepers prefer keeping more than one animal in the same habitat. While this requires careful thought, planning and execution on the part of the keeper, it is possible in some cases. However, beginners often underestimate the increased workload that multiple animals generate.

Many breeders and keepers house leopard tortoises in small groups. While generally acceptable, the process requires more work and forethought than is commonly used. Rather than simply acquiring a group of tortoises and placing them together in a cage, it is important that you consider the following issues:

- The tortoises must have all passed through individual quarantine periods and be free of pathogens before they are housed together. While quarantine cages need not be as large as the long-term home for the animals, they must still be large enough to allow the animals to thermoregulate and get enough exercise.

- Males may engage in combat during the breeding season, which can lead to serious injuries. Accordingly, the best strategy is to keep one male with several females.

- While you need not double the size of the enclosure for every tortoise you add to the colony, the total area must be large enough for all of the animals to create their own burrows and have enough room to exercise.

- Not all leopard tortoises will cohabitate amicably. For reasons that often escape the eyes of their human keepers, some tortoises will fight routinely. This phenomenon is not limited to males; females will occasionally exhibit antagonistic behaviors towards other females.

44

- Always observe new additions carefully for several weeks to ensure they are cohabitating well with the others in the cage. While the tortoises may all get along initially, the social dynamics of the colony may change over time.

Chapter 7: Establishing the Thermal Environment

Providing the proper thermal environment is one of the most important aspects of reptile husbandry. As ectothermic ("cold blooded") animals, leopard tortoises rely on the surrounding temperatures to regulate the rate at which their metabolism operates.

Providing a proper thermal environment can mean the difference between a healthy, thriving tortoise and one who spends a great deal of time at the veterinarian's office, battling infections and illness.

While individuals may demonstrate slightly different preferences, and different species have slightly different preferences, most active leopard tortoises prefer ambient temperatures in the mid- to high-80s Fahrenheit (about 30 to 32 degrees Celsius). Inactive (sleeping) tortoises prefer temperatures in the low 70s Fahrenheit (21 to 23 degrees Celsius).

While these are appropriate air temperatures for leopard tortoises, they will also require a basking spot during the day, with a temperature of about 90 to 100 degrees Fahrenheit (32 to 37 degrees Celsius).

Providing your tortoise with a suitable thermal environment requires the correct approach, the correct heating equipment and the tools necessary for monitoring the thermal environment.

Size-Related Heating Concerns

Before examining the best way to establish a proper thermal environment, it is important to understand that your tortoise's body size influences the way in which he heats up and cools off.

Because volume increases more quickly than surface area does with increasing body size, small individuals experience more rapid temperature fluctuations than larger individuals do.

Accordingly, it is imperative to protect small individuals from temperature extremes. Conversely, larger tortoises are more tolerant of temperature extremes than smaller individuals are (though they should still be protected from temperature extremes).

Thermal Gradients

In the wild, tortoises move between different microhabitats so that they can maintain ideal body temperature as much as possible.

The best way to do this is by clustering the heating devices at one end of the habitat, thereby creating a basking spot (the warmest spot in the enclosure).

The temperatures will slowly drop with increasing distance from the basking spot, which creates a *gradient* of temperatures. Barriers, such as branches and vegetation, also help to create shaded patches, which provide additional thermal options.

This mimics the way temperatures vary from one small place to the next in your pet's natural habitat. For example, a wild tortoise may move under some vegetation too cool off at midday, or move to a sunny location to warm up in the morning.

By establishing a gradient in the enclosure, your captive tortoise will be able to access a range of different temperatures, which will allow him to manage his body temperature just as his wild counterparts do.

Adjust the heating device until the surface temperatures at the basking spot are between 90 and 100 degrees Fahrenheit (32 to 37 degrees Celsius). Provide a slightly cooler basking spot for immature individuals, with maximum temperatures of about 92 degrees Fahrenheit (33 degrees Celsius).

Because there is no heat source at the other end of the cage, the ambient temperature will gradually fall as your tortoise moves away from the heat source. Ideally, the cool end of the cage should be in the low 70s Fahrenheit (22 degrees Celsius).

The need to establish a thermal gradient is one of the most compelling reasons to use a roomy cage. In general, the larger the cage, the easier it is to establish a suitable thermal gradient.

Heating Equipment

There are a variety of different heating devices you can use to keep your tortoise's habitat within the appropriate temperature range.

Be sure to consider your choice carefully, and select the best type of heating device for you and your tortoise.

Heat Lamps

Heat lamps are usually the best choice for supplying heat to your tortoise's habitat. Heat lamps consist of a reflector dome and an incandescent bulb. The light bulb produces heat (in addition to light) and the metal reflector dome directs the heat to a spot inside the cage.

You will need to clamp the lamp to a stable anchor or part of the cage's frame. Always be sure that the lamp is securely attached and will not be dislodged by vibration, children or pets.

Because fire safety is always a concern, and many keepers use high-wattage lightbulbs, opt for heavy-duty reflector domes with ceramic bases, rather than economy units with plastic bases. The price difference is negligible, given the stakes.

One of the greatest benefits of using heat lamps to maintain the temperature of your pet's habitat is the flexibility they offer. While you can adjust the amount of heat provided by heat tapes and other devices with a rheostat or thermostat, you can adjust the enclosure temperature provided by heat lamps in two ways:

- Changing the Bulb Wattage

The simplest way to adjust the temperature of your pet's cage is by changing the wattage of the bulb you are using.

For example, if a 40-watt light bulb is not raising the temperature of the basking spot high enough, you may try a 60-watt bulb. Alternatively, if a 100-watt light bulb is elevating the cage temperatures higher than are appropriate, switching to a 60-watt bulb may help.

- Adjusting the Distance between the Heat Lamp and the Basking Spot

The closer the heat lamp is to the cage, the warmer the cage will be. If the habitat is too warm, you can move the light farther from the enclosure, which should lower the basking spot temperatures slightly.

However, the farther away you move the lamp, the larger the basking spot becomes. It is important to be careful that you do not move it to far away, which will reduce the effectiveness of the thermal gradient by heating the enclosure too uniformly. In very large cages, this may not compromise the thermal gradient very much, but in a small cage, it may eliminate the "cool side" of the habitat.

In other words, if your heat lamp creates a basking spot that is roughly 1-foot in diameter when it is 1 inch away from the screen, it will produce a slightly cooler, but larger basking spot when moved back another 6 inches or so.

Ceramic Heat Emitters
Ceramic heat emitters are small inserts that function similarly to light bulbs, except that they do not produce any visible light – they only produce heat.

Ceramic heat emitters are used in reflector-dome fixtures, just as heat lamps are. The benefits of such devices are numerous:

- They typically last much longer than light bulbs do

- They are suitable for use with thermostats

- They allow for the creation of overhead basking spots, as lights do

- They can be used day or night

However, the devices do have three primary drawbacks:

- They are very hot when in operation

- They are much more expensive than light bulbs

- You cannot tell by looking if they are hot or cool. This can be a safety hazard – touching a ceramic heat emitter while it is hot is likely to cause serious burns.

Radiant Heat Panels
Quality radiant heat panels are a great choice for heating most reptile habitats, including those containing tortoises. Radiant heat panels are essentially heat pads that stick to the roof of the habitat. They usually feature rugged, plastic or metal casings and internal reflectors to direct the infrared heat back into the cage.

Radiant heat panels have a number of benefits over traditional heat lamps and under tank heat pads:

- They do not produce visible light, which means they are useful for both diurnal and nocturnal heat production. They can be used in conjunction with fluorescent light fixtures during the day, and remain on at night once the lights go off.

- They are inherently flexible. Unlike many devices that do not work well with pulse-proportional thermostats, most radiant heat panels work well with on-off and pulse-proportional thermostats.

The only real drawback to radiant heat panels is their cost: radiant heat panels often cost about two to three times the price of light- or heat pad-oriented systems. However, many radiant heat panels outlast light bulbs and heat pads, a fact that offsets their high initial cost over the long term.

Heat Pads
Heat pads are an attractive option for many new keepers, but they are not without drawbacks.

- Heat pads have a high risk for causing contact burns.

- If they malfunction, they can damage the cage as well as the surface on which they are placed.

- They are more likely to cause a fire than heat lamps or radiant heat panels are.

However, if installed properly (which includes allowing fresh air to flow over the exposed side of the heat pad) and used in conjunction with a thermostat, they can be reasonably safe. With heat pads, it behooves the keeper to purchase premium products, despite the small increase in price.

Heat Tape
Heat tape is somewhat akin to a "stripped down" heat pad. In fact, most heat pads are simply pieces of heat tape that have already been connected and sealed inside a plastic envelope.

Heat tape is primarily used to heat large numbers of cages simultaneously. It is generally inappropriate for novices, and requires the keeper to make electrical connections. Additionally, a thermostat is always required when using heat tape.

Historically, heat tape was used to keep water pipes from freezing – not to heat reptile cages. While some commercial heat tapes have been designed specifically for reptiles, many have not. Accordingly, it may be illegal, not to mention dangerous, to use heat tapes for purposes other than for which they are designed.

Heat Cables

Heat cables are similar to heat tape, in that they heat a long strip of the cage, but they are much more flexible and easy to use. Many heat cables are suitable to use inside the cage, while others are designed for use outside the habitat.

Always be sure to purchase heat cables that are designed to be used in reptile cages. Those sold at hardware stores are not appropriate for use in a cage.

Heat cables must be used in conjunction with a thermostat, or, at the very least, a rheostat.

Nocturnal Temperatures

Because leopard tortoises safely tolerate temperatures in the low-70s Fahrenheit (21 to 22 degrees Celsius) at night, most keepers can allow their pet's habitat to fall to ambient room temperature at night.

Because it is important to avoid using lights on your tortoise's habitat at night, those living in homes with lower nighttime temperatures will need to employ additional heat sources. Most such keepers accomplish this through the use of ceramic heat emitters.

Thermometers

It is important to monitor the cage temperatures very carefully to ensure your pet stays health. Just as a water test kit is an aquarist's best friend, quality thermometers are some of the most important husbandry tools for reptile keepers.

Ambient and Surface Temperatures

Two different types of temperature are relevant for pet tortoises: ambient temperatures and surface temperatures.

The ambient temperature in your animal's enclosure is the air temperature; the surface temperatures are the temperatures of the objects in the cage. Both are important to monitor, as they can differ widely.

Measure the cage's ambient temperatures with a digital thermometer. An indoor-outdoor model will feature a probe that allows you to measure the temperature at both ends of the thermal gradient at once. For example, you may position the thermometer at the cool side of the cage, but attach the remote probe to a branch near the basking spot.

Because standard digital thermometers do not measure surface temperatures well, use a non-contact, infrared thermometer for such measurements. These devices will allow you to measure surface temperatures accurately from a short distance away.

Thermostats and Rheostats

Some heating devices, such as heat lamps, are designed to operate at full capacity for the entire time that they are turned on. Such devices should not be used with thermostats – instead, care should be taken to calibrate the proper temperature by tweaking the bulb wattage.

Other devices, such as heat pads, heat tape and radiant heat panels are designed to be used with a regulating device, such as a thermostat or rheostat, which maintains the proper temperature

Rheostats

Rheostats are similar to light-dimmer switches, and they allow you to reduce the output of a heating device. In this way, you can dial in the proper temperature for the habitat.

The drawback to rheostats is that they only regulate the amount of power going to the device – they do not monitor the cage temperature or adjust the power flow automatically. In practice, even with the same level of power entering the device, the amount of heat generated by most heat sources will vary over the course of the day.

If you set the rheostat so that it keeps the cage at the right temperature in the morning, it may become too hot by the middle of the day. Conversely, setting the proper temperature during the middle of the day may leave the morning temperatures too cool.

Care must be taken to ensure that the rheostat controller is not inadvertently bumped or jostled, causing the temperature to rise or fall outside of healthy parameters.

Thermostats

Thermostats are similar to rheostats, except that they also feature a temperature probe that monitors the temperature in the cage (or under the basking source). This allows the thermostat to adjust the power going to the device as necessary to maintain a predetermined temperature.

For example, if you place the temperature probe under a basking spot powered by a radiant heat panel, the thermostat will keep the temperature relatively constant under the basking site.

There are two different types of thermostats:

- On-Off Thermostats

On-Off Thermostats work by cutting the power to the device when the probe's temperature reaches a given temperature. For example, if the thermostat were set to 85 degrees Fahrenheit (29 degrees Celsius), the heating device would turn off whenever the temperature exceeds this threshold. When the temperature falls below 85, the thermostat restores power to the unit, and the heater begins functioning again. This cycle will continue to repeat, thus maintaining the temperature within a relatively small range.

Be aware that on-off thermostats have a "lag" factor, meaning that they do not turn off when the temperature reaches a given temperature. They turn off when the temperature is a few degrees above that temperature, and then turn back on when the temperate is a little below the set point. Because of this, it is important to avoid setting the temperature at the limits of your pet's acceptable range. Some premium models have an adjustable amount of threshold for this factor, which is helpful.

- Pulse Proportional Thermostats

Pulse proportional thermostats work by constantly sending pulses of electricity to the heater. By varying the rate of pulses, the amount of energy reaching the heating devices varies. A small computer inside the thermostat adjusts this rate to match the set-point temperature as measured by the probe. Accordingly, pulse proportional thermostats maintain much more consistent temperatures than on-off thermostats do.

Lights should not be used with thermostats, as the constant flickering may stress your pet. Conversely, heat pads, heat tape, radiant heat panels and ceramic heat emitters should always be used with either a rheostat or, preferably, a thermostat to avoid overheating your pet.

Thermostat Failure

If used for long enough, all thermostats eventually fail. The question is will yours fail today or twenty years from now. While some thermostats fail in the "off" position, a thermostat that fails in the "on" position may overheat your tortoises. Unfortunately, tales of entire collections being lost to a faulty thermostat are too common.

Accordingly, it behooves the keeper to acquire high-quality thermostats. Some keepers use two thermostats, connected in series arrangement. By setting the second thermostat (the "backup thermostat") a few degrees higher than the setting used on the "primary thermostat," you safeguard yourself against the failure of either unit.

In such a scenario, the backup thermostat allows the full power coming to it to travel through to the heating device, as the temperature never reaches its higher set-point temperature.

However, if the first unit fails in the "on" position, the second thermostat will keep the temperatures from rising too high. The temperature will rise a few degrees in accordance with the higher set-point temperature, but it will not get hot enough to harm your pets.

If the backup thermostat fails in the "on" position, the first thermostat retains control. If either fails in the "off" position, the temperature will fall until you rectify the situation, but a brief exposure to relatively cool temperatures is unlikely to be fatal.

Chapter 8: Lighting the Enclosure

Sunlight plays an important role in the lives of most diurnal reptiles, including leopard tortoises.

It is always preferable to provide your pet with access to unfiltered sunlight, but this is not always possible. In these cases, it is necessary to provide your tortoise with high quality lighting, which can partially replace the light created by the sun.

leopard tortoises deprived of appropriate lighting may become seriously ill. Learning how to provide the proper lighting for reptiles is sometimes an arduous task for beginners, but it is very important to the long-term health of your pet that you do. To understand the type of light your tortoise needs, you must first understand a little bit about light.

The Electromagnetic Spectrum

Light is a type of energy that physicists call electromagnetic radiation; it travels in waves. These waves may differ in amplitude, which correlates to the vertical distance between consecutive wave crests and troughs, frequency, which correlates with the number of crests per unit of time, and wavelength.

Wavelength is the distance from one crest to the next, or one trough to the next. Wavelength and frequency are inversely proportional, meaning that as the wavelength increases, the frequency decreases. It is more common for reptile keepers to discuss wavelengths rather than frequencies.

The sun produces energy (light) with a very wide range of constituent wavelengths. Some of these wavelengths fall within a range called the visible spectrum; humans can detect these rays with their eyes. Such waves have wavelengths between about 390 and 700 nanometers. Rays with wavelengths longer or shorter than these limits are broken into their own groups and given different names.

Those rays with around 390 nanometer wavelengths or less are called ultraviolet rays or UV rays. UV rays are broken down into three different categories, just as the different colors correspond with different wavelengths of visible light. UVA rays have wavelengths between 315 to 400 nanometers, while UVB rays have wavelengths between 280 and 315 nanometers while UVC rays have wavelengths between 100 and 280 nanometers.

Rays with wavelengths of less than 280 nanometers are called x-rays and gamma rays. At the other end of the spectrum, infrared rays have wavelengths longer than 700 nanometers; microwaves and radio waves are even longer.

UVA rays are important for food recognition, appetite, activity and eliciting natural behaviors. UVB rays are necessary for many reptiles to produce vitamin D3. Without this vitamin, reptiles cannot properly metabolize their calcium.

Light Color

The light that comes from the sun and light bulbs is composed of a combination of wavelengths, which create the blended white light that you perceive. This combination of wavelengths varies slightly from one light source to the next.

The sun produces very balanced white light, while "economy" incandescent bulbs produce relatively fewer blue rays and yields a yellow-looking light. High-quality bulbs designed for reptiles often produce very balanced, white light. The degree to which light causes objects to look as they would under sunlight is called the Color Rendering Index, or CRI. Sunlight has a CRI of 100, while quality bulbs have CRIs of 80 to 90; by contrast, a typical incandescent bulb has a CRI of 40 to 50

Light Brightness

Another important characteristic of light that relates to tortoises is luminosity, or the brightness of light. Measured in units called Lux, luminosity is an important consideration for your lighting system. While you cannot possibly replicate the intensity of the sun's light, it is desirable in most circumstances to ensure the habitat is lit as well as is reasonably possible.

Without access to appropriately bright lighting, many reptiles become lethargic, depressed or exhibit hibernating behaviors. Dim lighting may inhibit feeding and cause tortoises to become stressed and ill.

However, while it is important to provide very bright lighting in portions of the cage, you must also provide the tortoises with shade, into which they can retreat if they desire.

Your Tortoise's Lighting Needs
To reiterate, leopard tortoises (and most other diurnal reptiles) require:

- Light that is comprised of visible light, as well as UVA and UVB wavelengths

- Light with a high color-rendering index

- Light of the sufficiently strong intensity

Now that you know what your tortoise requires, you can go about designing the lighting system for his habitat. Ultraviolet radiation is the most difficult component of proper lighting to provide, so it makes sense to begin by examining the types of bulbs that produce UV radiation.

The only commercially produced bulbs that produce significant amounts of UVA and UVB and suitable for a tortoise habitat are linear fluorescent light bulbs, compact fluorescent light bulbs and mercury vapor bulbs.

Neither type of fluorescent bulb produces significant amounts of heat, but mercury vapor bulbs produce a lot of heat and serve a dual function. In many cases, keepers elect to use both types of lights – a mercury vapor bulb for a warm basking site with high levels of UV radiation and fluorescent bulbs to light the rest of the cage without raising the temperature. You can also use fluorescent bulbs to provide the requisite UV radiation and use a regular incandescent bulb to generate the basking spot.

Fluorescent bulbs have a much longer history of use than mercury vapor bulbs, which makes some keepers more comfortable using them. However, many models only produce moderate amounts of UVB radiation. While some mercury vapor bulbs produce significant quantities of UVB, some question the wisdom of producing more UV radiation than the animal receives in the wild. Additionally, mercury vapor bulbs are much too powerful to use in small habitats, and they are more expensive initially.

Most fluorescent bulbs must be placed within 12 inches (25 centimeters) of the basking surface, while some mercury vapor bulbs should be placed farther away from the basking surface – be sure to read the manufacturer's instructions before use. Be sure that the bulbs you purchase specifically state the amount of UVB radiation they produce; this figure is expressed as a percentage, for example 7% UVB. Most UVB-producing bulbs require replacement every six to 12 months – whether or not they have stopped producing light.

However, ultraviolet radiation is only one of the characteristics that tortoise keepers must consider. The light bulbs used must also produce a sunlight-like spectrum. Fortunately, most high-quality light bulbs that produce significant amounts of UVA and UVB radiation also feature a high color-rendering index. The higher the CRI, the better, but any bulbs with a CRI of 90 or above will work well. If you are having trouble deciding between two otherwise evenly matched bulbs, select the one with the higher CRI value.

Brightness is the final, and easiest, consideration for the keeper to address. While no one yet knows what the ideal luminosity for a tortoise's cage is, it makes sense to ensure that part of the cage features very bright lighting. However, you should always offer a shaded retreat within the enclosure into which your tortoise can avoid the light if he desires.

Connect the lights to an electric timer to keep the length of the day and night consistent. Most leopard tortoises thrive with 12 hours of daylight and 12 hours of darkness all year long.

Chapter 9: Substrate and Furniture

Substrate choice is an important consideration for your leopard tortoise's enclosure. Although they don't burrow as frequently as some other tortoises, they may do so occasionally to escape oppressive temperatures or avoid detection by predators while they are sleeping.

Accordingly, the substrate must yield easily enough that the tortoises can dig into it, yet it must retain its structural integrity enough to permit the construction of stable tunnels.

Many different hobbyists and breeders swear by a given recipe for making the perfect leopard tortoise substrate. As long as such recipes contain no toxic or harmful types of soil, do not produce excess dust and allow the tortoises to burrow, they should all be acceptable.

Most such recipes feature varying amounts of play sand and either coconut fiber or organic topsoil. The sand helps to prevent the substrate from holding too much moisture and ensures adequate drainage, while the coconut fiber or soil has enough moisture and the proper type of structure, to maintain burrows.

It is a good idea to sift any substrates before placing them in your tortoise's pen to prevent including harmful items that may have made their way into the substrate, such as nails, sharp sticks or trash.

Provide at least 16 inches (40 centimeters) of soil, but it is preferable to provide 24 inches (60 centimeters) of depth or more. Tamp the soil down firmly before placing the tortoises in their cage.

Cage Furniture

To complete your leopard tortoise habitat, you must provide him with visual barriers and places to hide. You may also want to add things for aesthetic value and your own enjoyment.

Cork bark

The outer bark of the cork oak tree (*Quercus suber*), cork bark is available in both tubes and flat slabs. Tubes work best for tortoise maintenance, although you can come up with creative ways to use flat pieces in many cases.

The primary downsides to cork bark relate to its price (it is often rather expensive) and its tendency to collect debris in the cracks on its surface, which makes cleaning difficult.

Cardboard and Other Disposable Hides

Cardboard tubes, boxes or sheets also make excellent hiding spaces, as do sections of foam egg crate. These materials are light weight, very low cost and easy to replace once soiled. Try to arrange these items in ways that mimic some of the hiding places tortoises would use in the wild.

Plastic Containers

You can make functional – if not pretty – hides with inverted plastic containers that have a hole cut into the side to provide a door.

Plastic containers are an affordable choice, and they are quite easy to keep clean. However, it is important to pick containers that will provide a tight space in which your tortoise can hide, rather than a gigantic box, which won't provide the security your tortoise desires. It is also wise to use an opaque box, rather than a translucent one, for similar, security-related reasons.

Plants

Live plants may require more work and effort on the part of the keeper, but they offer a place for your pet to slip out of sight, and they look nice too.

Always wash all plants before placing them in the enclosure to help remove any pesticide residues. It is also wise to discard the potting soil used for the plant and replace it with fresh soil, which you know contains no pesticides, perlite or fertilizer.

While you can plant cage plants directly in soil substrates, this complicates maintenance and makes it difficult to replace the substrate regularly. Accordingly, it is generally preferable to keep the plant in some type of container. Be sure to use a catch tray under the pot, so that water draining from the container does not flow into the cage.

You must use care to select a species that will thrive in your tortoise's enclosure. This essentially means selecting plants that will thrive in a hot and somewhat dry climate. They must also be able to thrive in relatively low-light conditions, if you are keeping your pets indoors.

As much as is possible, choose plants that have broad leaves, which will allow them to serve as visual barriers for your tortoise.

Be aware that your tortoise may nibble on any plants included in the enclosure, so be sure to stick with non-toxic species.

Chapter 10: Maintaining the Captive Habitat

Now that you have acquired your tortoise and set up the enclosure, you must develop a protocol for maintaining his habitat. While tortoise habitats require major maintenance every month or so, they only require minor daily maintenance.

In addition to designing a husbandry protocol, you must embrace a record-keeping system to track your tortoise's growth and health.

Cleaning and Maintenance Procedures

Once you have decided on the proper enclosure for your pet, you must keep your tortoise fed, hydrated and ensure that the habitat stays in proper working order to keep your captive healthy and comfortable.

Some tasks must be completed each day, while others are should be performed weekly, monthly or annually.

Daily
- Monitor the ambient and surface temperatures of the habitat.

- Ensure adequate humidity if necessary, by misting the cage.

- Spot clean the cage to remove any loose insects, feces, urates or pieces of shed skin.

- Ensure that the lights, latches and other moving parts are in working order.

- Verify that your tortoise is acting normally and appears healthy. You do not necessarily need to handle him to do so.

- Feed your tortoise a plate of fresh vegetables (note that some keepers only feed their captives three or four times per week).

Weekly
- Change sheet-like substrates (newspaper, paper towels, etc.).

- Clean the inside surfaces of the enclosure.

- Inspect your tortoise closely for any signs of injury, parasites or illness.

- Wash and sterilize all food dishes.

Monthly
- Break down the cage completely, remove and discard particulate substrates in indoor cages.

- Stir substrate in outdoor cage if possible.

- Sterilize drip containers and similar equipment in a mild bleach solution.

- Measure and weigh your tortoise.

- Photograph your pet (recommended, but not imperative).

- Prune any plants as necessary.

Annually
- Replace the batteries in your thermometers and any other devices that use them.

- Replace UVB lights (some require replacement every six months)

Cleaning your tortoise's cage and furniture is relatively simple. Regardless of the way it became soiled, the basic process remains the same:

1. Rinse the object
2. Using a scrub brush or sponge and soapy water, remove any organic debris from the object.
3. Rinse the object thoroughly.
4. Disinfect the object.
5. Re-rinse the object.
6. Dry the object.

Chemicals & Tools
A variety of chemicals and tools are necessary for reptile care. Save yourself some time by purchasing dedicated cleaning products and keeping them in the same place that you keep your tools.

Spray Bottles
Misting your tortoise and his habitat with fresh water is one of the best ways to provide him with an appropriate humidity level. You can do this with a small, handheld misting bottle or a larger, pressurized unit (such as those used to spray herbicides). Automated

units are available, but they are rarely cost-effective unless you are caring for a large colony of animals.

Small Brooms

Small brooms are great for sweeping up small messes and bits of substrate. It is usually helpful to select one that features angled bristles, as they'll allow you to better reach the nooks and crannies of your pet's cage and the surrounding area.

Ideally, the broom should come with its own dust pan to collect debris, but there are plenty of work-arounds for those that don't come with their own.

Scrub Brushes or Sponges

It helps to have a few different types of scrub brushes and sponges on hand for scrubbing and cleaning different items. Use the least abrasive sponge or brush suitable for the task to prevent wearing out cage items prematurely. Do not use abrasive materials on glass or acrylic surfaces. Steel-bristled brushes work well for scrubbing coarse, wooden items, such as branches.

Spatulas and Putty Knives

Spatulas, putty knives and similar tools are often helpful for cleaning reptile cages. For example, urates (which are not soluble in anything short of hot lava) often become stuck on cage walls or furniture. Instead of trying to dissolve them with harsh chemicals, just scrape them away with a sturdy plastic putty knife.

Spatulas and putty knives can also be helpful for removing wet newspaper, which often becomes stuck to the floor of the cage.

Small Vacuums

Small, handheld vacuums are very helpful for sucking up the dust left behind from substrates. They are also helpful for cleaning the cracks and crevices around the cage doors. A shop vacuum, with suitable hoses and attachments, can also be helpful, if you have enough room to store it.

Steam Cleaners

Steam cleaners are very effective for sterilizing cages, water bowls and durable cage props after they have been cleaned. In fact, steam is often a better choice than chemical disinfectants, as it will not leave behind a toxic residue. Never use a steam cleaner near your tortoise, the plants in his cage or any other living organisms.

Soap
Use a gentle, non-scented dish soap. Antibacterial soap is preferred, but not necessary. Most people use far more soap than is necessary -- a few drops mixed with a quantity of water is usually sufficient to help remove surface pollutants.

Bleach
Bleach (diluted to one-half cup per gallon of water) makes an excellent disinfectant. Be careful not to spill any on clothing, carpets or furniture, as it is likely to discolor the objects.

Always be sure to rinse objects thoroughly after using bleach and be sure that you cannot detect any residual odor. Bleach does not work as a disinfectant when in contact with organic substances; accordingly, items must be cleaned before you can disinfect them.

Veterinarian Approved Disinfectant
Many commercial products are available that are designed to be safe for their pets. Consult with your veterinarian about the best product for your situation, its method of use and its proper dilution.

Avoid Phenols
Always avoid cleaners that contain phenols, as they are extremely toxic to some reptiles. In general, do not use household cleaning products to avoid exposing your pet to toxic chemicals.

Keeping Records
It is important to keep records regarding your pet's health, growth and feeding, as well as any other important details. In the past, reptile keepers would do so on small index cards or in a notebook. In the modern world, technological solutions may be easier.

You can record as much information about your pet as you like, and the more information to you record, the better. But minimally, you should record the following:

Pedigree and Origin Information
Be sure to record the source of your tortoise, the date on which you acquired him and any other data that is available. Breeders will often provide customers with information regarding the sire, dam, date of

birth, weights and feeding records, but other sources will rarely offer comparable data.

Feeding Information
Record the date of each feeding, as well as the type of food item(s) offered. It is also helpful to record any preferences you may observe or any meals that are refused.

It is also wise to record the times you supplement the food with calcium or vitamin powders, unless you employ a standard weekly protocol.

Weights and Length
Because you look at your pet frequently, it is difficult to appreciate how quickly he is (or isn't) growing. Accordingly, it is important to track his size diligently.

Weigh your tortoise with a high quality digital scale. It is often easiest to use a dedicated "weighing container" with a known weight to measure your pet. Simply subtract the weight of the container to obtain the weight of your tortoise.

You can measure your tortoise's length as well, but it is not as important as his weight.

Maintenance Information
Record all of the noteworthy events associated with your pet's care. While it is not necessary to note that you misted the cage each day, it is appropriate to record the dates on which you changed the substrate or sterilized the cage.

Whenever you purchase new equipment, supplies or caging, note the date and source. This not only helps to remind you when you purchased the items, but it may help you track down a source for the items in the future, if necessary.

Breeding Information
If you intend to breed your tortoises, you should record all details associated with pre-breeding conditioning, cycling, introductions, matings, color changes, copulations and egg deposition.

Record all pertinent information about any resulting clutches as well, including the number of viable eggs, as well as the number of unhatched and unfertilized eggs.

Additionally, if you keep several tortoises together in the same enclosure, you'll want to be careful to document the details of egg deposition, so you can be sure you know the correct parentage of each egg.

Record Keeping Samples
The following are two different examples of suitable recording systems.

The first example is reminiscent of the style employed by many with large collections. Because such keepers often have numerous animals, the notes are very simple.

The second example demonstrates a simple approach that is employed by many with small collections (or a single pet): keeping notes on paper.

Such notes could be taken in a notebook or journal, or you could type directly into a word processor. It does not matter *how* you keep records, just that you *do* keep records.

Number:	44522	Genus: Species:	Stigmachelys pardalis	Gender: DOB:	Male 3/20/14	CARD #2
6.30.15 Grass clippings	7.03.15 Grass clippings	7.07.15 Grass clippings	7.11.15 Grass clippings	7.15.15 Grass clippings		
7.01.15 Grass and flowers	7.05.15 Grass clippings	7.08.15 Greens and fruit	7.12.15 Greens and fruit	7.16.15 Sterilized Cage		
7.02.15 Greens and fruit	7.06.15 Grass and flowers	7.10.15 Weight: 485 grams	7.14.15 Grass and flowers			

Date	Notes
4-26-13	Acquired "Lola the Leopard Tortoise" from a breeder named Mark at the in-town reptile expo. Mark explained that Lola's scientific name is Stigmachelys pardalis. She cost $175. Mark said he purchased the turtle in March, but he does not know the exact date.
4-27-13	Lola spent the night in the container I bought her in. I purchased a small plastic storage box cage, a heat lamp and a thermometer at the hardware store, and I ordered a non-contact thermometer and full-spectrum light online. I added a small cardboard box so she had somewhere to hide.
4-28-13	Lola eagerly drank when I put a water dish in front of her. She was also hungry! She ate a huge plate of veggies in about 5 minutes.
4-29-13	I fed Lola another plate of greens today. She ate them as quickly as he ate the first.
4-30-13	Lola ate another big plate of food today.

Chapter 11: Feeding Leopard Tortoises

Feeding your leopard tortoise a healthy diet is one of the most important aspects of his care. This not only means providing your pet with suitable food items, but providing them in the proper way, in the appropriate amounts and on a proper schedule.

Different types of foods for your leopard tortoise are detailed below.

Grasses

Grasses should make up the bulk of your leopard tortoise's diet. Many of the grasses that are common in residential landscapes are edible, palatable and nutritious for tortoises.

- Alfalfa hay

- Timothy hay

- Bermuda grasses

- Fescue grasses

- Rye grasses

- Couch grass

- Buffalo grass

- Kikuyu grass

- Blue Grama grass

- Dallas grass

- Wintergrass

- Bluegrass

- Wheat grass

- Crab grass

- Tall oat grass

- Orchard grass

- Raspberry leaves and flowers (remove thorns)

Leaves, Weeds and Flowers

Grasses, leaves, weeds and flowers are also valuable food sources for your leopard tortoise, and they should be included as regular components of your turtle's food.

Unfortunately, such items are very difficult to come by, and you will likely be forced to harvest such plants from your back yard or some other place.

- Mulberry leaves

- Petunia leaves and flowers

- Dandelion leaves and flowers

- Hibiscus leaves and flowers

- Rose leaves and flowers

- Clover leaves and flowers

- Common sorrel

- Basil

- Prickly pear (with spines removed)

- Blackberry leaves and flowers (remove thorns)

- Squash blossoms

Grocery Store Vegetables

The grocery store is the easiest place to acquire food for your tortoise, but most of the foods are not appropriate for your pet. While some of the vegetables in the grocery store, such as endive, cactus pads and collard greens, can serve as regular components of your tortoise's menu, others are only appropriate when offered in moderation. Many of the common vegetables at the grocery store are very high in oxalic acid, phytic acid or phosphorus.

In some cases, farmer's markets and specialty grocery stores may stock vegetables that are more appropriate for leopard tortoises. For example, Greek and Mediterranean grocers often stock grape leaves, which are a great food source for your tortoise (be sure to only purchase fresh, freeze-dried or frozen grape leaves, not the pickled variety that comes packed in brine solution).

- Endive

- Kale

- Escarole

- Radicchio

- Squash (sparingly)

- Zucchini (sparingly)

- Cucumber (sparingly)

- Parsley (sparingly)

- Collard greens

- Turnip greens

- Radish greens

- Carrot greens

- Cactus pads (thorns removed)

- Banana leaves

- Dill weed (not all tortoises find this palatable)

- Lambs lettuce

- Arugula

- Cress

- Japanese radish greens

- Grape leaves

Fruits

You can provide your leopard tortoise with the occasional fruit treat, but they shouldn't form a significant portion of your pet's diet. The primary problem with fruits is that they have very high levels of water and sugar. When this sugar makes its way into the tortoise's digestive system, it often initiates a parasite population explosion, which can cause the tortoise to have intestinal distress.

- Apples (remove cores and seeds)

- Pears

- Blackberries

- Raspberries

- Honeydew Melon

- Cantaloupe

- Mango

- Figs

- Persimmons

Preparing Food for Your Tortoise

While a little dirt is unlikely to sicken your tortoise, it makes sense to keep their food as clean as possible. Bacteria, fungi and parasites likely litter the ground of your pet's enclosure, so use a clean food dish or flat rock for your pet's supplemental meals.

Obviously, your tortoise will still be eating many things off the enclosure floor (such as live grass or bales of hale, placed in the habitat), so make every effort to keep the pen tidy.

Some keepers prepare "feeding trays" for their pets, which help to keep your pet from eating off the ground. To do so, fill several small, shallow trays with sterilized, organic potting soil. Then plant edible grass and plant seeds in the soil; after sprouting, place the tray in with your tortoise, who can then feed on the tender, young plants. You will need to make several such trays and rotate them regularly if this is to be an important food source.

While it is not strictly necessary to do so, most keepers cut or shred foods for small tortoises to make it easier for them to eat. However, this is more important for some foods than it is for others. For example, even the smallest hatchlings can handle live grasses, hibiscus leaves and flowers, but coarse vines and hay are difficult for small tortoises to handle.

Feeding Frequency

The proper feeding frequency for your tortoise depends on his size, species and age. Generally speaking, tortoises should be fed four to seven times per week; the younger the tortoise, the more often it should be fed.

As long as your tortoise is healthy, gets plenty of exercise, has access to suitable temperatures and is provided with a wide variety of food items, you do not have to worry about over-feeding him during the first few years of life. However, mature animals – or those living in small cages – may become overweight if fed too frequently.

Ultimately, you must adjust your tortoise's diet by monitoring his weight regularly. Young tortoises should exhibit steady, moderate growth rates, while mature animals should maintain a relatively consistent body weight.

If your tortoise fails to grow or begins losing weight, you must increase the frequency of his feedings. Conversely, those that gain excessive wait should be placed on restrictive diets. Consult with your veterinarian before altering your feeding schedule drastically.

Vitamin and Mineral Supplements

Many keepers add commercially produced vitamin and mineral supplements to their pet's food on a regular basis. In theory, these supplements help to correct dietary deficiencies and ensure that captive tortoises get a balanced diet. In practice, things are not this simple.

While some vitamins and minerals are unlikely to build up to toxic levels, others may very well cause problems if provided in excess. This means that you cannot simply apply supplements to every meal – you must decide upon a sensible supplementation schedule.

Because the age, sex and health of your pet all influence the amount of vitamins and minerals your pet requires, and each individual product has a unique composition, it is wise to consult your veterinarian before deciding upon a supplementation schedule.

However, most keepers provide vitamin supplementation once each week, and calcium supplementation several times per week.

Despite the best efforts of tortoise keepers to feed their pets a nutritious, well-balanced diet, it is a very hard task to accomplish. To help offset potential deficiencies, many tortoise keepers supplement the diet of their turtles with extra minerals and vitamins.

Usually, such supplements come in powder or liquid form, and they are designed to be mixed in with a tortoise's food or given orally. For obvious reasons, it is easier to mix supplements into your tortoise's food, rather than try to coax him to open his mouth.

Most keepers use two different types of supplement: a multivitamin and a calcium powder. Sometimes, calcium powders are also fortified with vitamin D3 to ensure that the tortoise can properly metabolize the calcium. Vitamins and calcium powder are best kept separate from each other to allow for differential doses.

The proper dosages of vitamins and calcium are poorly understood. If a tortoise receives too much supplementation of either vitamins or calcium it can lead to serious health problems. To be safe, discuss your tortoise's needs with your veterinarian to arrive at a safe dosage schedule. Although hypercalcaemia (too much calcium in the bloodstream) is much rarer than hypocalcaemia (too little calcium in the bloodstream), it is a possibility worth considering when devising a calcium supplementation schedule. While hypocalcaemia causes a number of potential health problems, hypercalcaemia can cause serious health problems as well, including renal failure.

Generally speaking, most tortoise keepers provide vitamin supplements once per week. Calcium supplementation varies based on the age and gender of your tortoise. Young, quickly growing tortoises and reproductively active females require more calcium than adult males do.

When females are producing eggs, they require very high levels of calcium. Without enough, their health may be in danger as well as the health of the developing offspring. To help reduce the chances of a problem, many keepers place cuttlebones in a female's habitat during the breeding season, with the hope that the female will supplement her own diet as necessary. Many tortoises ignore cuttlebones throughout the year, but then consume nearly the entire bone over the course of a day or two, as the time for egg deposition approaches. Cuttlebones have the additional benefit of helping to keep your tortoise's beak from becoming overgrown.

If your tortoise is housed outside, it is unlikely that he is deficient in vitamin D3, so opt for a calcium powder without it. By contrast, even though indoor tortoises should be provided with UVB lighting to help them produce their own vitamin D3, they likely do not produce enough to metabolize all of their calcium.

Chapter 12: Providing Water to Your Tortoise

Like all other animals, leopard tortoises require water to survive. Proper hydration is critical for the health of these animals, so most keepers provide fresh drinking water to their tortoises, and some even provide their tortoises with periodic baths, to further ensure they remain hydrated.

Drinking Water

Wild leopard tortoises obtain much of their water through the plants they consume, but they also drink from puddles and streams when the opportunity arises. Accordingly, you'll want to provide fresh drinking water for your pet.

The easiest way to provide them with water is via a large, flat, shallow dish. Avoid deep, narrow water containers, as they are difficult for the tortoises to access and more likely to spill. Additionally, because tortoises are not strong swimmers, it is imperative to avoid offering water in a dish deep enough to cause the turtles to drown.

Plastic plant saucers, cat litter pans and plastic storage boxes make effective water dishes for adults, while small glass saucers, storage box lids or commercial water dishes designed for small tortoises work best for young leopard tortoises.

Always keep the water clean to prevent your tortoise from becoming sick. Wash the water dish every day with soap and water, but be sure to rinse it thoroughly before returning it to the enclosure. It is also wise to disinfect the water dish periodically by soaking it in a mild bleach solution for 1 hour and then rinsing it well.

Some keepers prefer to offer water periodically (perhaps twice or thrice per week) rather than keeping a water dish in the cage at all times. This helps to keep the enclosure from becoming too damp, but, as long as the enclosure has adequate ventilation, a water dish will probably not increase the humidity of the enclosure too undesirable levels.

Many keepers use tap water for their tortoises, but others prefer to use bottled spring water instead. It is possible that some of the chemicals found in tap water are harmful for your pet, so consult with your veterinarian before using tap water for your pet's drinking needs.

Soaking

In addition to providing drinking water, many tortoise keepers soak their tortoises periodically in a small bit of water. This helps to ensure they remain hydrated and often helps to dislodge dirt, grime or food stuck to the bottom of their shell.

Soak your tortoise by adding a small amount of water to a plastic storage container, bucket or similar enclosure. Only add enough water to wet the bottom of the tortoise's shell – never make your tortoise swim or struggle to keep his head above the water. This equates to about ¼ to ½ inch for hatchlings, and 1 to 2 inches for large adults.

Avoid using water that is substantially warmer or cooler than your pet's body temperature. One easy way to accomplish this is by placing the soaking container (with lukewarm water already added) into your pet's enclosure for about an hour before soaking him. This way, the water will be roughly the same temperature as the ambient temperatures in the cage, which will prevent your pet from becoming chilled or burned.

A typical soaking regimen may call for you to soak your tortoise for 20 minutes, twice per week, although some keepers provide soaks more or less frequently than this. In all cases, it is important to monitor your tortoise while he is soaking to avoid accidents.

Note that your tortoise may defecate in the water. If this happens, you must change the water immediately to prevent your pet from drinking the contaminated water.

Dry your turtle off with paper towels after soaking him, which will help keep the substrate from sticking to his shell.

Humidity

Leopard tortoises live in areas with low to moderate humidity levels, but they spend lots of time in deep burrows and clumps of vegetation, where the relatively humidity is actually quite high.

However, leopard tortoises will not thrive in enclosures that are kept continually humid. This may lead to skin lesions and respiratory infections. Accordingly, it is important for tortoise owners to provide their tortoises with access to both low- and high-humidity areas within their enclosure.

The best way to do this is by providing one or more humid hiding places, into which your tortoise can retreat. You can keep such places damp by periodically sprinkling a little water under the hiding container. This is especially important for young tortoises, who may begin "pyramiding" when deprived of a high-humidity retreat.

Chapter 13: Interacting with Your Tortoise

You must be sure that your interactions with your turtle are safe and positive for all parties involved. Contact with a large predator (such as yourself) may cause the turtle stress, which can lead to illness and maladaptation. Additionally, improper handling can cause your pet to suffer injuries.

In general, this means that you should avoid most unnecessary physical contact with your pet. This is especially true with leopard tortoises, as they are a shy species, which does not respond to handling as well as leopard tortoises and a few other species do.

However, you need to observe your turtle for signs of illness regularly, and this will occasionally necessitate directly handling or manipulating the animal.

While it is relatively easy to handle a small leopard tortoise, handling a large adult requires a bit more care. Not only are large individuals heavier than small ones, they may wiggle about while you are holding them, potentially causing you to drop your tortoise. Even falls from only a few inches off the ground can cause serious injuries, so you must use great care when lifting your pet.

Handling Your Tortoise

Different techniques are necessary for handling tortoises of different sizes. Hatchlings are relatively easy to hold, but large adults require entirely different techniques.

Suspending a turtle by its tail can lead to spinal injuries; never use a turtle's tail to support its bodyweight, regardless of its size.

The best way to hold these very small turtles is by placing your index finger on top of the animal's carapace and placing your thumb under its plastron. Do not pinch the shell too firmly, as young turtle shells lack the rigidity of adult shells.

Larger leopard tortoises require two hands to keep their body supported. Place the thumb of each hand on the top or sides of the turtle's carapace, and place the remaining fingers on the turtle's plastron, between the front and back legs.

Transporting Your Pet

From time to time, it will be necessary to transport your pet. When doing so, you must keep the turtle protected from injury, within the appropriate temperature range and protected from sources of stress.

The best way to do so is by placing your turtle in a large plastic storage box, filled with a soft layer of newspaper or hay. Opaque boxes will keep your turtle calmer, while transparent boxes will allow you to observe the animal without opening the lid.

Be sure to drill a few ventilation holes on each of the container's vertical sides so that your pet can breathe easily. When drilling the holes, drill from the inside of the tub toward the outside, to prevent any sharp edges from contacting your turtle.

Hygiene

Turtles often carry various strains of *Salmonella* bacteria, as well as other harmful pathogens. While these bacteria rarely cause illness in the turtles, they can make humans – particularly those with compromised immune systems – very ill. In tragic cases, death can result from such infections.

Accordingly, it is imperative to employ sound hygiene practices when caring for a pet turtle. In general, this means:

- Always wash your hands with soap and warm water following any contact with your pet, the enclosure or items that have contacted either.

- Never wash turtle cages, furniture or tools in sinks or bathtubs used by humans.

- Never perform any husbandry tasks in kitchens or bathrooms used by humans.

- Keep high-risk individuals, such as those who are less than 5 years of age, elderly, pregnant or otherwise immunocompromised, away from captive turtles and their habitats.

Chapter 14: Common Health Concerns

Like many other tortoises, leopard tortoises are remarkably hardy animals, who often remain healthy despite their keeper's mistakes. In fact, most illnesses that befall pet tortoises result from improper husbandry, and are therefore, entirely avoidable.

Nevertheless, like most other reptiles, leopard tortoises often fail to exhibit any symptoms that they are sick until they have reached an advanced state of illness. This means that prompt action is necessary at the first hint of a problem. Doing so provides your pet with the greatest chance of recovery.

While proper husbandry is solely in the domain of the keeper, and some minor injuries or illnesses can be treated at home, veterinary care is necessary for many health problems.

Finding a Suitable Vet

While any veterinarian – even one who specializes in dogs and cats – may be able to help you keep your pet happy, it is wise to find a veterinarian who specializes in treating reptiles. Such veterinarians are more likely to be familiar with your pet species and be familiar with the most current treatment standards for reptiles.

Some of the best places to begin your search for a reptile-oriented veterinarian include:

- Veterinary associations

- Local pet stores

- Local colleges and universities

It is always wise to develop a relationship with a qualified veterinarian before you need his or her services. This way, you will already know where to go in the event of an emergency, and your veterinarian will have developed some familiarity with your pet.

When to See the Vet

Most conscientious keepers will not hesitate to seek veterinary attention on behalf of their pet. However, veterinary care can be expensive for the keeper and stressful for the kept, so unnecessary visits are best avoided.

If you are in doubt, call or email your veterinarian and explain the problem. He or she can then advise you if the problem requires an office visit or not.

However, you must always seek prompt veterinary care if your pet exhibits any of the following signs or symptoms:

- Traumatic injuries, such as lacerations, burns, broken bones, cracked shells or puncture wounds

- Sores, ulcers, lumps or other deformations of the skin

- Intestinal disturbances that do not resolve within 48 hours

- Drastic change in behavior

- Inability to deposit eggs

Remember that reptiles are perfectly capable of feeling pain and suffering, so apply the golden rule: If you would appreciate medical care for an injury or illness, it is likely that your pet does as well.

Common Health Problems

The following are some of the most common health problems that afflict tortoises. Be alert for any signs of the following maladies, and take steps to remedy the problem.

Respiratory Infections

Respiratory infections are some of the most common illnesses that afflict turtles and other captive reptiles.

The most common symptoms of respiratory infections are discharges from the nose or mouth; however, lethargy, inappetence and behavioral changes (such as basking more often than normal) may also accompany respiratory infections.

Myriad causes can lead to this type of illness, including communicable pathogens, as well as, ubiquitous, yet normally harmless, pathogens, which opportunistically infect stressed animals.

Your turtle may be able to fight off these infections without veterinary assistance, but it is wise to solicit your vet's opinion at the first sign of illness. Some respiratory infections can prove fatal and require immediate attention.

Your vet will likely obtain samples, send of the samples for laboratory testing and then interpret the results. Antibiotics or other medications may be prescribed to help your turtle recover, and your veterinarian will likely encourage you to keep the turtle's stress level low, and ensure his enclosure temperatures are ideal.

In fact, it is usually a good idea to raise the temperature of the basking spot upon first suspecting that your turtle is suffering from a respiratory infection. Elevated body temperatures (such as those that occur when mammals have fevers) help the turtle's body to fight the infection, and many will bask for longer than normal when ill.

Metabolic Bone Disease
Metabolic bone disease (MBD) is a complicated phenomenon that befalls turtles who are provided with insufficient calcium or insufficient amounts of the active form of vitamin D (D3), which is necessary for calcium utilization.

A well-rounded, diverse diet with plenty of grasses and weeds helps to ensure your pet receives enough calcium. Additionally, many keepers supplement their turtle's food items with calcium powders. However, it is important to consult with your veterinarian to devise a suitable supplementation schedule, as providing too much calcium can be just as problematic as providing too little.

A balanced diet will provide your turtle with plenty of inactive vitamin D. To allow your pet to convert this into the active form, you must provide it with exposure to ultraviolet radiation (specifically UVB). This can be accomplished either by housing your turtle outdoors and allowing them to bask in natural sunlight, or by illuminating their enclosure with full spectrum lights that produce light in the UVB portion of the spectrum.

When deprived of proper lighting, the calcium levels in the turtle's blood fall. This causes the turtle's body to draw calcium from the bones (including the shell) to rectify the problem.

As calcium is removed from the bones, they become soft and flexible, rather than hard and rigid. This can lead to broken bones or disfigurement, which can leave your turtle unable to eat, walk or swim.

Advanced cases of MBD are rarely treatable, and euthanasia is often the only humane option. However, when caught early and treated aggressively, some of the symptoms of the disease can be stopped. Accordingly, it is of the upmost importance to seek veterinary care at the first sign of MBD.

Pyramiding

Tortoise keepers use the term "pyramiding" to refer to the improper growth and development of a tortoise's scutes. Often, each scute takes on a pyramid-like shape, being wide at the bottom, narrow at the top and significantly raised, rather than lying flat. The result is a bumpy, rather than smooth, carapace.

The condition's cause was initially thought to be related to a poor diet, rich in animal protein. While animal-based food sources are not healthy for tortoises, research has shown that diets rich in animal products do not cause this particular malady.

Currently, most of the available evidence points to water and hydration levels as being the most important factor in causing pyramiding. It appears that chronic dehydration during the turtle's early years causes the scutes to form abnormally.

Accordingly, it is important to provide young tortoises with a humid retreat, in which they will spend considerable amounts of time. This mimics the wild lifestyle of leopard tortoises; although they live in very dry environments, their burrows remain relatively humid, which keeps the turtles from dehydrating.

Pyramiding is permanent once it occurs, so it is of paramount importance to provide young tortoises with the correct husbandry.

Shell Rot

Shell rot is a catchall term for a variety of maladies related to a turtle's shell. Shell rot normally takes the form of lesions or ulcers; sometimes, a small amount of fluid may leak from the wounds.

Shell rot may occur because of a systematic infection or as a local phenomenon. Bacteria or fungi may be the primary cause of the problem, or injuries may provide an opportunity for pathogens to colonize the tissues.

Shell rot is usually treatable with prompt veterinary care, so always see your veterinarian at the first sign of problems.

Parasites

Parasites are rare among captive-bred tortoises, but poor husbandry can cause them to become a problem. Parasites rarely become problematic for wild turtles, unless they become injured, stressed or ill.

Most internal parasites cause intestinal problems, such as runny or watery stools, vomiting or decreased appetites. Your veterinarian can collect blood or stool samples from your turtle, analyze them to determine what parasites, if any, are present, and prescribe medications to clear the infestation. Often, multiple treatments are necessary to eradicate the parasites completely.

External parasites afflict leopard tortoises on occasion, usually in the form of ticks. Because some ticks carry dangerous diseases, you should have your veterinarian inspect any animal carrying the parasitic arthropods.

Anorexia

Leopard tortoises are normally ravenous eaters, who rarely pass up the chance to consume calories. However, they may refuse food if ill, if kept in suboptimal temperatures (including seasonally cool temperatures, such as occur during the winter) or are preoccupied by breeding.

Refusing a meal or two is not cause for alarm, but if your turtle refuses food for longer than this, be sure to review your husbandry practices. If the turtle continues to refuse food without an obvious reason for doing so, consult your veterinarian.

Injuries

Despite their protective shells and armored legs, leopard tortoises can become injured in myriad ways, including battles with cagemates, overly zealous breeding attempts, or by sustaining burns from heaters. While tortoises are likely to heal from most minor wounds without medical attention, serious wounds will necessitate veterinary assistance.

Your vet will likely clean the wound, make any repairs necessary (shell patches, sutures, etc.) and prescribe a course of antibiotics to help prevent infection. Be sure to keep the enclosure as clean as possible during the healing process.

Egg Binding

Egg binding occurs when a female is unable or unwilling to deposit her eggs in a timely fashion. If not treated promptly, death can result.

The primary symptoms of egg binding are similar to those that occur when a gravid turtle approaches parturition. Egg bound turtles may dig to create an egg chamber or attempt to escape their enclosure. However, unlike turtles who will deposit eggs normally, egg bound turtles continue to exhibit these symptoms without producing a clutch of eggs.

As long as you are expecting your turtle to lay eggs, you can easily monitor her behavior and act quickly if she experiences problems. However, if you are not anticipating a clutch, this type of problem can catch you by surprise.

Prolapse

Prolapses occur when a turtle's intestines protrude from its vent. This is an emergency situation that requires prompt treatment. Fortunately, intestinal prolapse is not terribly common among tortoises.

You will need to take the animal to the veterinarian, who will attempt to re-insert the intestinal sections. Sometimes sutures will be necessary to keep the intestines in place while the muscles regain their tone.

Try to keep the exposed tissue damp, clean and protected while traveling to the vet. It is likely that this problem is very painful for the animal, so try to keep its stress level low during the process.

Quarantine
Quarantine is the practice of isolating animals to prevent them from transferring diseases between themselves.

If you have no other pet reptiles (particularly turtles), quarantine is unnecessary. However, if you already maintain other turtles you must provide all new acquisitions with a separate enclosure.

At a minimum, quarantine all new acquisitions for 30 days. However, it is wiser still to extend the quarantine period for 60 to 90 days, to give yourself a better chance of discovering any illness present before exposing your colony to new, potentially sick, animals. Professional zoological institutions often quarantine animals for six months to a year. In fact, some zoos keep their animals in a state of perpetual quarantine.

Chapter 15: Breeding Leopard Tortoises

Many – if not most – turtle keepers are eventually bitten by the captive breeding bug. Determined to produce a clutch of adorable hatchlings, these keepers acquire specimens of each sex and begin waiting for eggs.

This is a natural progression for keepers, and, when carried out in responsible fashion, breeding can be beneficial for the species, as captive breeding projects help alleviate pressure on wild populations.

However, irresponsible breeders often cause serious problems for the hobby.

Such breeders often set out with the explicit goal of profiting from their turtles, rather than enjoying their pets in their own right. This ensures failure for the vast majority of people that try to breed turtles for profit.

Pre-Breeding Considerations

Before you set out to breed leopard tortoises, consider the decision carefully. Unfortunately, few keepers realize the implications of breeding their turtles before they set out to do so.

Ask yourself if you will be able to:

- Provide adequate care for a pair of adult turtles

- Provide the proper care for the female while gravid

- Afford emergency veterinary services if necessary

- Incubate the eggs in some type of incubator

- Provide housing for the hatchlings

- Provide food for the hatchlings

- Dedicate the time to caring for the hatchlings

- Find new homes for the hatchlings

- If you cannot answer each of these questions affirmatively, you are not in a position to breed tortoises responsibly.

Legal Issues

Before deciding to breed tortoises, you must investigate the relevant laws in your area. Some municipalities require turtle breeders to obtain licenses, insurance and permits, although others do not.

Finally, be aware that it is illegal to buy or sell turtles with carapaces less than 4 inches in length in the United States, except for educational or scientific purposes.

Sexing Tortoises

If, after considering the proposition carefully, you decide to breed tortoises, you will need at least one sexual pair of animals. To be sure that you have a sexed pair, you must be able to distinguish one sex from the other.

The easiest way to distinguish the sex of a leopard tortoise is by observing the tails and anal scutes of the animals. Males have much longer, thicker tails than females do, and their anal scutes are wider than those of females.

Pre-Breeding Conditioning

Once you have obtained a sexual pair, you must begin conditioning them for breeding. This is important because animals that are not in very good condition may not be able to handle the rigors of cycling and breeding.

Take the turtles to visit your veterinarian, who will be able to ascertain their health status. Some veterinarians may only perform a visual inspection, but others may collect biological samples for additional testing.

If your vet determines that your turtles are not healthy, take whatever steps are recommended to rectify the problem before commencing breeding trials.

Once you are certain that your turtles are in good health, it is time to initiate your breeding protocols.

Cycling

Cycling is a term used to describe the practice of providing captive reptiles with an annual variation in temperature (or other factors, such as photoperiod). The concept seeks to mimic the natural seasonal cycle and synchronize the reproductive cycle of the reptiles in question.

In some species, proper cycling appears to be necessary for successful reproduction in captivity, while other species reproduce quite successfully with no variation in temperature or any other factor. Because most leopard tortoise breeders maintain their animals outdoors, they are already exposed to a natural seasonal cycle.

Wild leopard tortoises typically breed between May and October when the temperatures are warm. Captives in the United States often breed during this same time, especially when they've been provided with 6 to 8 weeks of "winter" temperatures to synchronize their reproductive cycles.

You should not expose leopard tortoises to very low temperatures during the cycling period. Leopard tortoises do not hibernate or bromate, so you need to avoid making them deal with temperatures that are too low for them to tolerate.

Typically, cycling regimens involve reducing the photoperiod to 10 hours of light per day, keeping the day time temperatures under 80 degrees and allowing the nighttime temperatures to drop into the low 70s.

However, it is important to note that because leopard tortoises inhabit a large swath of Africa, different populations establish different breeding cycles. Accordingly, you may need to experiment with different schedules and cycling regimens to achieve success.

Mating

When it is time to end the cycling regimen and introduce the tortoises to each other, proceed slowly. For the first several days, the tortoises may not eat and may only bask for a short period of time. Allow them to wake at their own rate, and provide food as they begin to show interest. A month or so after becoming active, the males will begin pursuing females. It is also at this time that the males are most likely to engage in combat, so monitor them carefully. Despite their harmless appearance, tortoises can bite each other savagely, causing serious bodily harm to the other animal.

Mating is not always a gentle affair, and the males may bite at the female's heads while trying to get them to accept their advances. They may mate more than one time, but one mating is usually sufficient for fertilization. However, males may attempt to mate with females repeatedly. If this is allowed to go on for an extended time, it can cause the females great stress. The best solutions are to either remove the males for a few weeks until they calm down and then reintroduce them to the communal cage, or incorporate more females in the cage to spread out the stress.

Gravid

Shortly after successful copulation, suitably healthy females become gravid. Unlike many other reptiles, turtles do not offer very many signs to indicate their reproductive condition.

Manual palpation, which is a common method for determining the reproductive condition of many other reptiles, is rarely helpful with turtles. In fact, attempting to feel a female's eggs with your fingers may cause them to rupture. Accordingly, it is wise to avoid the practice entirely. Instead, the best clues lie in the female's behavior.

Many gravid females reduce their food intake as their eggs develop and take up more space in their body cavity. They may also begin to explore their surroundings and look for a suitable place to dig their eggs.

Nevertheless, the only way to be certain that your turtle is gravid is by having your veterinarian perform an x-ray. This will not only verify that she is holding eggs, but it will allow you to know approximately how many eggs she is carrying.

Egg Deposition

As the time for egg deposition nears, the female will become increasingly restless. She may pace for long periods of time or even look for a way to escape from the enclosure.

At this point, the female is seeking out a place to dig a nest and deposit her eggs. Hopefully, you have designed the enclosure so that such a place is always available, but, if you have not, you must provide her with a place she finds suitable.

Typically, leopard tortoises look for a warm, sunny, sloping area, with a substrate suitable for nest construction. They prefer an area of exposed dirt, rather than having to dig through grass or vegetation.

Ideally, the egg-deposition site should have a footprint of at least two to three times the size of the turtle's shell and contain substrate as deep as the turtle's shell is long.

If your female does not find the provided site to her liking, you will need to tweak it until she feels comfortable. This can mean loosening the substrate, compacting the substrate, providing a greater depth of substrate or moving the egg deposition site to another location in the enclosure.

This is often a challenging component of turtle breeding, and even highly experienced zookeepers occasionally have problems devising a suitable egg-laying site.

If your turtle cannot find a suitable place to lay her eggs, she may scatter the eggs in the enclosure or retain them internally. Usually, these outcomes lead to health problems for the female, such as dystocia (egg binding).

Assuming that your turtle finds the egg deposition area suitable, she will eventually crawl into it, dig a small depression and fill it with eggs. After completing the process, she will cover the hole and leave the area. It can be very difficult to locate a nest site afterwards, so do your best to mark the location during, or immediately after, parturition.

Egg Incubation

Keepers employ any of several different strategies for incubating tortoise eggs. No one method is "correct," although artificially incubating the eggs in a climate-controlled container usually leads to the greatest success.

The least labor-intensive approach is to leave the eggs where they are and let them incubate naturally. After all, leopard tortoises have been incubating their eggs in just this way for millions of years.

However, doing so is unlikely to lead to a high rate of success, as you have little control over the temperatures of the mass. Additionally, the eggs may be vulnerable to predators, including rodents or fire ants.

You will need to be very observant for emerging hatchlings, which may make their way out of the nest over the course of a month or more. Hatchlings may be crushed by the adults very easily, so you should remove them as quickly as possible.

If you would prefer more control of the incubation process, you can excavate the egg chamber, remove the eggs and place them in a climate-controlled incubator for the remainder of their development.

Leopard tortoise eggs are relatively robust, and tolerate a wide range of incubation temperatures; however, temperatures between 82 and 86 degrees Fahrenheit (27 to 30 degrees Celsius) lead to the best results. However, the incubation period can vary significantly. Some clutches hatch in as little as five months, while others may require more than a year.

This probably occurs because some leopard tortoise eggs pass through a state of stalled development called diapause. While breeders are still working out the details, it appears that some eggs can be coaxed into developing more quickly by altering the temperatures to interrupt the pause. To do so, most breeders expose the eggs to temperatures between 65 and 70 degrees Fahrenheit (18 to 21 degrees Celsius) for about a month, before restoring normal incubation temperatures.

Use great care when excavating the egg chamber to prevent damaging the eggs. Once you have accessed the eggs, mark the top of each with a graphite pencil. This will allow you to maintain the correct orientation when transferring the eggs to the incubator; inverting the eggs can cause the embryos to drown.

Avoid separating any eggs that have adhered to each other. While it is often possible to do so without damaging the eggs, such attempts should be left to those who have considerable experience incubating reptile eggs.

Egg Boxes

Egg boxes are small plastic storage boxes designed to hold the eggs inside the incubator. While their use is not always necessary in the strictest sense, they make it easier to maintain the climate surrounding the eggs.

Virtually any type of small plastic storage box will suffice, but consider a few things before selecting your egg boxes:

- Be sure to select boxes that are tall enough to contain 1 or 2 inches (2.5 to 5 centimeters) of incubation media as well as the eggs, which will rest on top of the media (partially buried).

- Whenever possible, select transparent egg boxes so that you can observe the eggs without having to open them.

- If possible, select boxes with domed lids, which will help prevent condensation from dripping on the eggs.

You will need to make two small holes (approximately one-quarter-inch or one-half centimeter in diameter) in each box to allow for air exchange inside the egg boxes.

Some breeders prefer to monitor the temperature of the egg boxes, while others prefer to monitor the temperature of the incubator. Either method will work, although if you desire to measure the temperatures inside the egg boxes, you will need to drill additional holes to accept a temperature probe.

You can select relatively large egg boxes so that they will accommodate large clutches, or you can use relatively small egg boxes, so that you can split up the clutch into several different sub groups.

Incubation Media

Several different incubation media are appropriate for egg incubation. Soil, soil and sand mixtures and vermiculite are some of the most common choices by breeders. Vermiculite works for a wide variety of reptile eggs, as it is quite easy to attain a suitable moisture level.

The substrate not only provides a protective cushion that supports the eggs, but it also provides moisture, which will keep the relative humidity of the egg box high. This will prevent the eggs from desiccating.

Too much humidity or dampness, however, can have a negative effect on the eggs, so it is important to keep enough water in the egg boxes, but not too much.

Many keepers strive to maintain humidity levels of 80 percent in the egg chamber, but others simply watch the eggs and adjust the humidity accordingly. If the eggs begin to exhibit wrinkles, they are drying out and more water is necessary. Conversely, if they begin to swell or exude fluid, the humidity should be lowered.

Some authorities recommend specific ratios of water and vermiculite, but as vermiculite absorbs water from the air, it is impossible to know how saturated the vermiculite was when you started.

Accordingly, the best approach is to judge the moisture with your hands. Beginning with dry vermiculite, slowly add water while stirring the mixture. The goal is to dampen the vermiculite just enough that it clumps when compressed in your hand. However, if water drips from the media when you squeeze it, the vermiculite is too damp.

The Incubator

You can either purchase a commercially produced incubator or construct your own. However, most beginning breeders are better served by purchasing a commercial incubator than making their own.

Commercial Incubators

Commercial egg incubators come in myriad styles and sizes. Some of the most popular models are similar to those used to incubate poultry eggs (these are often available for purchase from livestock supply retailers).

These incubators are constructed from a large foam box, fitted with a heating element and thermostat. Some models feature a fan for circulating air; while helpful for maintaining a uniform thermal environment, models that lack these fans are acceptable.

You can place an incubation medium directly in the bottom of these types of incubators, although it is preferable to place the media (and eggs) inside small plastic storage boxes, which are then placed inside the incubator.

These incubators are usually affordable and easy to use, although their foam-based construction makes them less durable than most premium incubators are.

Other incubators are constructed from metal or plastic boxes; feature a clear door, an enclosed heating element and a thermostat. Some units also feature a backup thermostat, which can provide some additional protection in case the primary thermostat fails.

These types of incubators usually outperform economy, foam-based models, but they also bear higher price tags. Either style will work, but, if you plan to breed turtles for many years, premium models usually present the best option.

Homemade Incubators

Although incubators can be constructed in a variety of ways, using many different materials and designs, two basic designs are most common.

The first type of homemade incubator consists of a plastic, glass or wood box, and a simple heat source, such as a piece of heat tape or a low-wattage heat lamp. The heating source must be attached to a thermostat to keep the temperatures consistent. A thermometer is also necessary for monitoring the temperatures of the incubator.

Some keepers make these types of incubators from wood, while others prefer plastic or foam. Although glass is a poor insulator, aquariums often serve as acceptable incubators; however, you must purchase or construct a solid top to retain heat.

Place a brick on the bottom of the incubator, and place the egg box on top of the brick, so that the eggs are not resting directly on the heat tape. The brick will also provide thermal mass to the incubator, which will help maintain a more consistent temperature.

The other popular incubator design adds a quantity of water to the design to help maintain consistent temperatures and a higher humidity. To build such a unit, begin with an aquarium fitted with a glass or plastic lid.

Place a brick in the bottom of the aquarium and add about two gallons of water to the aquarium; ideally, the water level should stop right below the top of the brick.

Add an aquarium heater to the water and set the thermostat to the desired temperature. Place the egg box on the brick, insert a temperature probe into the egg box and cover the aquarium with the lid (you may need to purchase a lid designed to allow the cords to pass through it).

This type of incubator works by heating the water, which will in turn heat the air inside the incubator, which will heat the eggs. Although it can take several days of repeated adjustments to get these types of incubators set to the exact temperature you would like, they are very stable once established.

Neonatal Husbandry

Observe the hatchlings as they emerge from their shells. Some turtles will remain in their shells for several days while they absorb the rest of their egg yolk. This is perfectly normal, and you should not remove such turtles from their eggs. Allow the turtle to absorb the entire yolk and exit the egg on his own.

A young leopard tortoise.

If for some reason, the egg becomes destroyed (such as through the activities of the clutchmates), move the turtle into a clean, plastic container with about 1/4 inch of water in the bottom. Do not pull the yolk free, and try to keep it from drying out.

Once the turtles have hatched and absorbed their egg yolk, they are ready to move to the nursery. The nursery container should be constructed from a small plastic storage box (you can split the clutch among several different boxes to reduce the stress on the hatchlings).

Drill or melt a few small ventilation holes in the top (always making sure the holes are drilled from the inside toward the outside to prevent any sharp edges from injuring the hatchlings) and place a few layers of paper towels on the bottom.

Add a very shallow water dish to the center of the cage (a 3-inch plant saucer works well) and keep it full of clean water. Leave the hatchlings inside the nursery for at least 24 hours to ensure they have absorbed their egg yolks are have become active.

Once a turtle has become active, you can move it to its "permanent" home. You can house a few hatchlings together in the same habitat, but avoid overcrowding them, which can lead to squabbles and injuries. Be sure there are more places to hide than there are turtles in the tank.

You can begin feeding them almost immediately after placing them in their new homes, but many will not begin feeding for a few days.

Chapter 16: Further Reading

Never stop learning more about your new pet's natural history, biology and captive care. This is the only way to ensure that you are providing your new leopard tortoise with the highest quality of life possible.

It's always more fun to watch your tortoise than read about him, but by accumulating more knowledge, you'll be better able to provide him with a high quality of life.

Books
Bookstores and online book retailers offer a treasure trove of information that will advance your quest for knowledge. While books represent an additional cost involved in reptile care, you can consider it an investment in your pet's well-being. Your local library may also carry some books about leopard tortoises, which you can borrow for no charge.

University libraries are a great place for finding old, obscure or academically oriented books about leopard tortoises. You may not be allowed to borrow these books if you are not a student, but you can view and read them at the library.

Herpetology: An Introductory Biology of Amphibians and Reptiles
By Laurie J. Vitt, Janalee P. Caldwell
Academic Press, 2013

Understanding Reptile Parasites: A Basic Manual for Herpetoculturists & Veterinarians
By Roger Klingenberg D.V.M.
Advanced Vivarium Systems, 1997

Infectious Diseases and Pathology of Reptiles: Color Atlas and Text
Elliott Jacobson
CRC Press

Designer Reptiles and Amphibians
Richard D. Bartlett, Patricia Bartlett

Magazines

Because magazines are typically published monthly or bi-monthly, they occasionally offer more up-to-date information than books do. Magazine articles are obviously not as comprehensive as books typically are, but they still have considerable value.

Reptiles Magazine
www.reptilesmagazine.com/
Covering reptiles commonly kept in captivity.

Practical Reptile Keeping
http://www.practicalreptilekeeping.co.uk/
Practical Reptile Keeping is a popular publication aimed at beginning and advanced hobbies. Topics include the care and maintenance of popular reptiles as well as information on wild reptiles.

Websites

The internet has made it much easier to find information about reptiles than it has ever been.

However, you must use discretion when deciding which websites to trust. While knowledgeable breeders, keepers and academics operate some websites, many who maintain reptile-oriented websites lack the same dedication to scientific rigor.

Anyone with a computer and internet connection can launch a website and say virtually anything they want about tortoises. Accordingly, as with all other research, consider the source of the information before making any husbandry decisions.

The Reptile Report
www.thereptilereport.com/
The Reptile Report is a news-aggregating website that accumulates interesting stories and features about reptiles from around the world.

Kingsnake.com
www.kingsnake.com

After starting as a small website for gray-banded kingsnake enthusiasts, Kingsnake.com has become one of the largest reptile-oriented portals in the hobby. The site features classified advertisements, a breeder directory, message forums and other resources.

The Vivarium and Aquarium News
www.vivariumnews.com/
The online version of the former print publication, The Vivarium and Aquarium News provides in-depth coverage of different reptiles and amphibians in a captive and wild context.

Journals
Journals are the primary place professional scientists turn when they need to learn about tortoises. While they may not make light reading, hobbyists stand to learn a great deal from journals.

Herpetologica
www.hljournals.org/
Published by The Herpetologists' League, Herpetologica, and its companion publication, Herpetological Monographs cover all aspects of reptile and amphibian research.

Journal of Herpetology
www.ssarherps.org/
Produced by the Society for the Study of Reptiles and Amphibians, the Journal of Herpetology is a peer-reviewed publication covering a variety of reptile-related topics.

Copeia
www.asihcopeiaonline.org/
Copeia is published by the American Society of Ichthyologists and Herpetologists. A peer-reviewed journal, Copeia covers all aspects of the biology of reptiles, amphibians and fish.

Nature
www.nature.com/

Although Nature covers all aspects of the natural world, many issues contain information that tortoise enthusiasts are sure to find interesting.

Supplies

You can obtain most of what you need to leopard tortoises through your local pet store, big-box retailer or hardware store, but online retailers offer another option.

Just be sure that you consider the shipping costs for any purchase, to ensure you aren't "saving" yourself a few dollars on the product, yet spending several more dollars to get the product delivered.

Big Apple Pet Supply
http://www.bigappleherp.com
Big Apple Pet Supply carries most common husbandry equipment, including heating devices, water dishes and substrates.

LLLReptile
http://www.lllreptile.com
LLL Reptile carries a wide variety of husbandry tools, heating devices, lighting products and more.

Doctors Foster and Smith
http://www.drsfostersmith.com
Foster and Smith is a veterinarian-owned retailer that supplies husbandry-related items to pet keepers.

Support Organizations

Sometimes, the best way to learn about tortoises is to reach out to other keepers and breeders. Check out these organizations, and search for others in your geographic area.

The National Reptile & Amphibian Advisory Council
http://www.nraac.org/
The National Reptile & Amphibian Advisory Council seeks to educate the hobbyists, legislators and the public about reptile and amphibian related issues.

American Veterinary Medical Association

www.avma.org

The AVMA is a good place for Americans to turn if you are having trouble finding a suitable reptile veterinarian.

The World Veterinary Association

http://www.worldvet.org/

The World Veterinary Association is a good resource for finding suitable reptile veterinarians worldwide.

References

Anderson, S. P. (2003). The Phylogenetic Definition of Reptilia. *Systematic Biology*.

Coulson, A. H. (1999). The growth pattern of the African tortoise Geochelone pardalis and other chelonians. *Canadian Journal of Zoology*.

DOWNS, M. K. (2006). DO SEASONAL AND BEHAVIORAL DIFFERENCES IN THE USE OFREFUGES BY THE LEOPARD TORTOISE (GEOCHELONE PARDALIS) FAVOR PASSIVE THERMOREGULATION? *Herpetologica*.

Milton, S. (1992). Plants eaten and dispersed by adult leopard tortoises Geochelone partlalis (Reptilia: Chelonii) in the southern Karoo . *South African Journal of Zoology*.

MK, M. (n.d.). The status and ecology of the Leopard Tortoise (Geochelone pardalis) on the farmland in the Nama-Karoo. *National Research Foundation*.

Paolo Galeotti, e. a. (2005). Do Mounting Vocalisations in Tortoises Have a Communication Function? A Comparative Analysis. *The Herpetological Journal*.

Printed in Great Britain
by Amazon